Cambridge English

MINDSET

FOR IELTS

An Official Cambridge IELTS Course

TEACHER'S BOOK **2**

Cambridge University Press
www.cambridge.org/elt
Cambridge English Language Assessment
www.cambridgeenglish.org

Cambridge University Press is part of the University of Cambridge.

It furthers the University's mission by disseminating knowledge in the pursuit of
education, learning and research at the highest international levels of excellence.

www.cambridge.org
Information on this title: www.cambridge.org/9781316640265

© Cambridge University Press and UCLES 2017

First published 2017
20 19 18 17 16 15 14 13 12 11 10 9 8 7 6 5 4 3 2 1

Printed in Dubai by Oriental Press

A catalogue record for this publication is available from the British Library

Additional resources for this publication at **www.cambridge.org/mindset**

About the author

Natasha De Souza

Natasha has been involved in the ELT industry for 15 years – as a teacher, Director of Studies, Examiner and an Examinations Officer. She started teaching IELTS in 2006, when she worked on a University Pathway and Foundation Programme for a language school in Cambridge. More recently, as a Director of Studies and an Examinations Officer, she was responsible for giving guidance to students and teachers on how the IELTS test works and how best to prepare for it.

The authors and publishers would like to thank the following people for their work on this level of the Student's Book.

Bryan Stephenson and Jock Graham for their editing and proof reading.

Design and typeset by emc design.

Audio produced by Leon Chambers at The Soundhouse Studios, London.

The publishers would like to thank the following people for their input and work on the digital materials that accompany this level.

Dr Peter Crosthwaite; Jeremy Day; Natasha de Souza; Ian Felce; Amanda French; Marc Loewenthal; Rebecca Marsden; Kate O'Toole; Emina Tuzovic; Andrew Reid; N.M.White.

Cover and text design concept: Juice Creative Ltd.

Typesetting: emc design Ltd.

Cover illustration: MaryliaDesign/iStock/Getty Images Plus.

CONTENTS

Student's Book

Mindset for IELTS Level 2 is aimed at students who are at B2 level and want to achieve a Band 6 or 6.5 result at IELTS. You can follow the book by topic and teach it lineally or alternatively you can focus on the different skills and papers that you would like your students to improve. It is designed for up to 90 hours of classroom use, but you be can be flexible and focus on key areas of your choice. The topics have been chosen based on common themes in the IELTS exam and the language and skills development is based on research in the corpus, by looking at the mistakes that students at this level commonly make in IELTS.

Mindset for IELTS Level 2 offers a flexible way of teaching. You can work through the units consecutively or choose the lessons that are important to your students. You can choose to teach the book by topic or by skill.

- Topics have been chosen to suit the needs and abilities of students at this level, they are topics that occur in the IELTS test, but are tailored to the needs and interests of your students.
- There is full coverage of the test both here and in the online modules. However, there is an emphasis on the parts of the exam where students aiming at a Band 6 or Band 6.5 will be able to pick up the most marks, maximising their chances of getting the score that they need.
- Each level of *Mindset* is challenging, but doesn't push students above what they can do.
- Grammar and vocabulary is built into the development of skills, so students improve their language skills as well as the skills that they need to learn to achieve the desired band score.

How *Mindset for IELTS* helps with each skill

- **Speaking** – *Mindset* gives you strategies for what happens if you don't know much of the topic. It also helps build vocabulary for each part of the test and allows students to grow in confidence.
- **Writing** – *Mindset* gives you tips on how to plan better and develop your ideas. There is coverage of all types of Task 1 and Task 2 and detailed help on how to approach each as well as model answers.
- **Reading** – Strategies for dealing with Reading texts on difficult and unknown topics are developed, as well as coverage of all question types. Strategies for improving reading skills in general as well as skills needed in the exam, such as an awareness of distraction and the use of paraphrases.
- **Listening** – *Mindset* gives coverage of all the Listening tasks, but concentrates on how your students can maximise their score. Vital skills for dealing with the paper like paraphrasing are developed and listening strategies that will help your students in everyday life are developed.

Outcomes

At the start of every lesson you will see a list of outcomes.

WRITING

IN THIS UNIT YOU WILL LEARN HOW TO

- select and compare key features of charts, graphs and tables

- structure an answer which compares information from charts, graphs and tables

- revise the form and use of comparatives.

In the Teacher's Book you will see how these outcomes relate to the lesson and the skills that your students need to develop in order to be successful in developing their English language and exam skills. There are typically three or four outcomes per lesson and look at skills that can be used both in the IELTS test and in their broader English language development; an IELTS strategy for dealing with a particular paper and a linguistic outcome that helps with vocabulary and grammar development.

Tip Boxes and Bullet Boxes

- Tip boxes help you and your students improve task awareness and language skills. You will find further information on how to get the most out of them in the Teacher's Book. Note that the number in the corner relates to the exercise that the tip goes with.

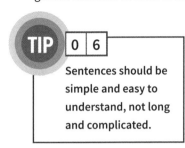

TIP 0 6

Sentences should be simple and easy to understand, not long and complicated.

- Bullet boxes tell you how the test works and how to get a better understanding of the test task being addressed.

Questions which require an answer of just a few words, like those in exercise 7, are a common feature of the exam. These are known as *short-answer* questions and they ask about factual details.

Teacher's Book

The Teacher's Book has been designed to help you teach the material effectively and to allow you to see how the language and skills development relate directly to the IELTS test. You will also find the following:

- Extension exercises – exercises that help you give your students more practice with key skills.
- Alternative exercises – ideas that you can use to make the exercises more relevant for your students.
- Definitions – to help you with some of the key terms that are used in IELTS.

How to use the online modules

As well as the students book there are several online modules that each provide 6-8 hours of further study. These can be used for homework or to reinforce what has been studied in the classroom. The core modules are:

- **Reading**
- **Listening**
- **Writing**
- **Speaking**
- **Grammar and Vocabulary**

In the Reading and Listening modules there is more practice with the same skills that they have studied but based on a different topic.

The Writing module builds on the skills that they have learnt in the unit and offers advice and model answers to help improve writing skills.

The Speaking module builds on knowledge of the topics that students have studied in the Student's book. This helps them to speak about the different topics with confidence and to develop the skills for the various parts of the Speaking Test. You can also see videos of students taking the test and complete exercises around this.

The Grammar and Vocabulary module reinforces and extends the vocabulary and grammar that has been studied in each unit of the book.

There are also a number of other online modules with specific learners in mind:

- **Chinese Pronunciation and Speaking**
- **Speaking Plus**

These modules look at the types of mistakes that students make at this level and from different language groups. The syllabus and exercises have been developed with insights from our corpus database of students speaking. Each module takes between **6 – 8 hours**. Students can also analyse and view video content of Speaking Tests in these modules.

- **Arabic Spelling and Vocabulary**
- **Arabic Writing**

- **Chinese Spelling and Writing**
- **Writing Plus**

These modules use our database of past writing IELTS papers and Corpus research to look at the typical mistakes that students from the different language groups make on the Writing paper of the exam. They are encouraged to improve their writing skills and also avoid the common pitfalls that students make. Each of these modules provides **6-8 hours of study**.

- **Academic Study Skills**

The University Skills Module helps to bridge the gap between the skills that students learn studying IELTS and the ones that they need for the exam. The module shows students how they can use the knowledge they have and what they will need to work on when going to study in an English Language context for Higher Education.

About the IELTS Academic Module

Academic Reading

The Reading paper is made up of three different texts, which progress in level of difficulty. There is a total of 40 questions. Candidates have one hour to complete the information, this includes the time needed to transfer answers to the answer sheet. There is no extra time for this. Each question is worth one mark.

The texts are authentic and academic, but written for a non-specialist audience. Candidates must use information that appears in the text to answer the questions. They cannot use outside knowledge if they know about the topic. The types of texts are similar to the texts that you may find in a newspaper or magazine, so it is important for your students to get as much reading of these types of text as possible.

Texts sometimes contain illustrations. If a text contains technical terms a glossary will be provided.

The different task types are:

Multiple choice	Candidates will be asked to choose **one** answer from **four** options; choose **two** answers from **five** options or choose **three** answers from **seven** options.
Identifying information (True / False / Not Given)	Say if a statement given as a fact is True / False or Not Given.
Identifying the writer's views or claims (Yes / No / Not Given)	Say if a statement agrees with the opinions of the author or if it is not given in the text.
Matching information	Match information to paragraphs in a text.
Matching headings	Match a heading from a list to the correct part of the text.
Matching features	Match a list of statements to a list of possible answers (e.g. specific people or dates).
Matching sentence endings	Complete a sentence with a word or words from the text inside the word limit which is given.
Sentence completion	Complete a sentence with a word or words from the text inside the word limit which is given.
Notes/Summary/Table/Flow- chart completion	Complete with a suitable word or words from the text.
Labelling a diagram	Label a diagram with the correct word or word from a text. The words will be given in a box of possible answers.
Short-answer questions	Answer questions using words from the text inside the word limit

Academic Writing

There are two separate writing tasks. Candidates must answer both tasks.

Task 1

- Candidates should spend 20 minutes on this task.
- Candidates should write a minimum of 150 words. They will be penalised if they write less.
- Candidates need to describe and summarise a piece of visual information. The information may be presented in a diagram, map, graph or table.

Task 2

- Candidates should spend 40 minutes on this task.
- Candidates should write a minimum of 250 words. They will be penalised if they write less.
- Candidates need to write a discursive essay. They will be given an opinion, problem or issue that they need to respond to. They may be asked to provide a solution, evaluate a problem, compare and contrast different ideas or challenge an idea.

Listening

The Listening Paper is made up of four different texts. There are a total of 40 questions and there are 10 questions in each section. The paper lasts for approximately 30 minutes and students are given an extra 10 minutes to transfer their answers to the answer sheet. Each question is worth one mark.

In **Part 1** Candidates will hear a conversation between two people about a general topic with a transactional outcome (e.g. someone booking a holiday, finding out information about travel, returning a bought object to a shop).

In **Part 2** Candidates will hear a monologue or prompted monologue on a general topic with a transactional purpose (e.g. giving information about an event)

In **Part 3** Candidates will hear a conversation between two or three people in an academic setting (e.g. a student and a tutor discussing a study project)

In **Part 4** Candidates will hear a monologue in an academic setting (e.g. a lecture)

There may be one to three different task types in each section of the paper the task types are:

Notes/Summary/Table/Flow-chart completion	Complete with a suitable word or words from the recording.
Multiple choice	Candidates will be asked to choose **one** answer from **three** alternatives or **two** answers from **five** alternatives.
Short-answer questions	Answer questions using words from the recording inside the word limit
Labelling a diagram, plan or map	Label a diagram/plan or map with a suitable word or words by choosing from a box with possible answers
Classification	Classify the given information in the question according to three different criteria (e.g. dates, names, etc.)
Matching	Match a list of statements to a list of possible answers in a box (e.g. people or dates)
Sentence completions	Complete a sentence with a word or words from the word limit which is given.

Speaking

The test is with an examiner and is recorded. The interview is made up of three parts.

Part 1

- Lasts for 4–5 minutes
- Candidates are asked questions on familiar topics like their hobbies, likes and dislikes.

Part 2

- Lasts for 3–4 minutes
- Candidates are given a task card with a topic (e.g. describe a special meal you have had) and are given suggestions to help them structure their talk. They have one minute to prepare their talk and then need to speak between 1 and 2 minutes on the topic.

Part 3

- Lasts for 4–5 minutes
- The examiner will ask candidates more detailed and more abstract questions about the topic in Part 2 (e.g. How are eating habits in your country now different from eating habits in the past)

In the Speaking test candidates are marked on Fluency and Coherence; Lexical Resource; Grammatical Range; Pronunciation.

What your students will need to do to get the band they require

Academic Reading

Candidates need to score approximately between 23 and 29 to obtain a Band 6 or 6.5 on Academic Reading.

Listening

Candidates need to score approximately between 23 and 29 to obtain a Band 6 or Band 6.5 on Listening.

Academic Writing and Speaking

The Public version of the IELTS Band Descriptors are available on www.ielts.org. To obtain a Band 6 students will need to illustrate all of the features of Band 6 and to obtain a Band 6.5 they will have to demonstrate all of the features of Band 6 and some of the features of Band 7.

How to connect knowledge of English language with the exam

Students beginning this course will already have a good knowledge of English. It is important to let them know that this existing knowledge will be very useful for the IELTS exam and will form the basis of developing further language knowledge and skills. The grammar, vocabulary and pronunciation they have already learned can be linked to different parts of the exam. In this book we help the student to do this.

Vocabulary

Vocabulary is a key component in all four papers in the exam and at this level, students are expected to have a fairly wide range of vocabulary. In this course, students are encouraged to build on their existing vocabulary by expanding on what they already know. For example, candidates are shown that when recording a new item of vocabulary, they should also think about the following: synonyms, lexical sets and recording in context.

Definitions

Synonyms- a word or phrase that means the same as another word or phrase

Lexical sets- a group of words which share the same topic or features e.g table, chair

Recording in context- to record a word, within a sentence or phrase.

e.g went I went to the doctors.

An awareness of synonyms is very important, as many of the tasks, across all papers, rely greatly on students knowing different words for the same thing. Furthermore, encouraging students to think in terms of lexical sets, will help them to expand their vocabulary in each topic area discussed. Finally, encouraging students to record new words in context, will ensure that they are used correctly. This is particularly important in the Speaking and Writing Papers when students are assessed on their production of vocabulary.

Grammar

At this level your students should be familiar with the majority of tenses/ grammatical structures. As each learner is different however, and their may be gaps in their grammatical knowledge, this course seeks to revise and compare some of the useful structures, necessary for the exam.

A revision of tenses, related to the past, present and future is useful for all four papers. For the productive skills, speaking & writing, the production of grammatical structures is particularly important. In part 1 of the writing for example, students must have a good knowledge of the passive in order to complete a task on describing a process. For the receptive skills (listening & reading) the emphasis is more on students understanding the meaning of the grammar being used.

Pronunciation

At this level, your students will already be fairly competent in the area of pronunciation. In other words, they will be generally understood when they speak. In order for your students to achieve a higher mark, this course aims to build on this, by introducing aspects such as intonation and sentence/ word stress, features which help a speaker sound more natural and comprehensible. For example, by encouraging students to use intonation, they are also able to communicate emotion as well as meaning.

How to prepare your own materials for IELTS

There are many IELTS practice materials available, both in bookshops and online, however you may want to create your own.

Reading

You can use texts from a number of sources: general English textbooks, the internet or texts you have written yourself. One important point to keep in mind however, is that the level of these texts must be pitched at the level of the students or the level they are aiming for, depending where you are in the course. If the readings are too difficult, students may be unable to complete any of the tasks given to them and/or be left feeling despondent. In order to check the level of a text you can use an online tool called, "English Profile."

As demonstrated throughout this course, skimming and scanning are two key skills needed for the Reading Paper. In order to practise and encourage the use of both these techniques in a freer way, you could try some of the following:

Give groups of students the same reading text and ask them to race to find the information- they could do this using a text you have created, another textbook or online.

Tell students to skim read a text quickly and then retell the main information to their partner.

Give groups of students different texts and ask them to write questions/ a quiz for other students. The groups then swap texts/ questions and scan the texts for the answers, under a time limit.

Listening

For your own listening material, you can also use recordings from other textbooks, record audios yourself or use online material. One of the easiest ways to produce your own listening material however, is to simply dictate role-plays or monologues to students.

Definition

Dictate: to say or read something for someone to write down

Using dictation means you can adapt the speed of your listening to suit the needs of your class. You can also ask the students to dictate the audio material, which they can also create, if you wanted.

Writing

For writing task 1, students need to write about graphs or a process. For this task you or the students, could easily create graphs based on information/data, which is of interest or personal to the class. For example, if the students were interested in a particular hobby, such as cycling, they could use data on this to create their own charts/ graphs etc..

For a process diagram, you can demonstrate the language needed for this task, by showing students a simple process using realia.

Definition

Realia: real objects or pieces of writing, used to help teach students in a class

For example, you could demonstrate the simple process of making a paper aeroplane using a piece of paper. You could also ask your students to demonstrate a process of their choice to the class.

For Part 2 of the writing you could exploit the use of sample answers found online, from other books or from the students themselves (with their permission) With these sample answers you could do some of the following:

cut them into sections and ask students to order appropriately(useful when teaching structure and coherence)

ask students to discuss what the sample answer does well and where it could be improved.

ask students to rewrite a sample essay from an opposing view

Speaking

For the Speaking Part of the test, you can write your own questions or ask your students to create questions they think will appear in this part of the exam. This will also help you to gauge their understanding of the Speaking exam.

General

When producing your own materials, it is important to ask yourself the following:

- Is this material the correct level for my students?
- Will it engage my students? (personalizing the topic is often a good way to do this)
- Are the instructions for the task clear and simple? (making the task over complicated can often deter from the main aim of the task)

READING

OUTCOMES

- skim a text quickly to understand the general idea
- scan a text for specific information to answer short-answer questions
- use skimming and scanning to locate the answer quickly
- understand and produce paraphrasing
- use the present continuous and present simple correctly.

OUTCOMES

Ask students to focus on the outcomes of the lesson. Elicit/ explain to students that *skimming* and *scanning* are both reading techniques, which are very useful for the exam. Timing is a major factor in the IELTS reading and therefore students need to be able to locate information quickly. Explain that these two techniques are designed to help with this. You do not need to discuss their meaning in detail at this stage, as each is described and practised fully, throughout the lesson.

Tell students that the theme of the unit is *The Man- Made Environment* and elicit meaning (anything in the environment made by people- more commonly buildings, but you could also have man-made beaches/lakes etc.)

This unit will focus on buildings or more specifically, homes. This is a popular topic in the exam and can arise in any of the four papers (reading, writing, speaking & listening).

LEAD-IN

01 To engage students in the topic/generate vocabulary, draw students' attention to the photos of houses on pages 8 & 9. Ask students if they would like to live in either of these houses? Why/ why not? What would be their ideal home and why?

Alternative

Choose your own selection of photos displaying different types of houses (big, small, old, modern etc.) and display on the board.

As the whole class discuss one of the photos -

e.g. What are the main features of the house? What do you like/dislike about the house?

Students then work in pairs to discuss all of the photographs in this way.

Feedback as a whole class and write any new vocabulary on the board.

Ask students to read the list of vocabulary and complete the table in exercise 01.

If needed, complete the first line of the table as a whole class.

Location: beach, city centre, mountains, countryside, remote island
Building type: skyscraper, bungalow, mansion, castle, garage
Style: glamorous, simple, traditional, modern, spacious
Rooms: cellar, gym, dining room
Parts of a room: staircase, floor, ceiling, window
Materials: wood, marble, leather, stone

02 Ask students to think about their dream home and complete Exercise 02. You could start this by providing a longer example and describe your own dream home.

As a whole class ask some of the students to report on what their partner has told them.

Definition

Skimming: to read a text quickly in order to understand the main idea.

Scanning: to read a text quickly in order to find specific information.

These techniques are useful for the exam because candidates need to be able to read texts quickly. Many candidates make the mistake of reading texts word for word. There is not time for this, as they have 60 minutes to answer 40 questions.

Tell students to read through the definition of skimming and scanning.

Ask students if they have used these techniques before. Elicit why they are important for the IELTS exam.

03 Write the words *scanning* and *skimming* on the board and elicit a few examples of when they are used, e.g. looking up a word in a dictionary- scanning. Write at least one example under each heading.

2 skimming	3 skimming	4 scanning
5 scanning	6 skimming	

Draw students' attention to *Tip 3,* which advises them to practise these reading techniques as much as possible, as this will help them greatly with the set time limit.

Practising these techniques in their mother-tongue as well as in English, may also help. They could do this at home by reading magazines, newspapers, books etc.

Extension

Devise a set of questions around the textbook, asking students to find information using skimming and scanning techniques. You could divide the class into teams and assign a point to whichever team produces the answer first.

E.g. In Unit 3, which page has an article on .... (skimming)

Read the article on page..... .How many .... (scanning)

Before locating the answer, students must also tell you which reading technique they will be using to find the information.

04 Ask students to look at the photograph of a home, which cost more than one billion dollars to build. Students discuss what they like/dislike about the design.

05 Explain to students that they are going to skim read an article about this home, to understand the main ideas. Set a time limit.

Draw students' attention to *Tip 5,* which reminds students to ignore unknown words.

> **Advice**
>
> It is a good idea not to permit the use of dictionaries during this and some other reading practice, as it is tempting for students to look up every unknown word. In preparation for the exam, students need to be accustomed to not having access to a dictionary.

06 Tell students to complete the questions in *Exercise 06.*

> **sample answer**
> 1 names, verbs, adjectives, numbers
> 3 Antilia (Mumbai, India)
> 4 1 f 2 d 3 c 4 e 5 g 6 a 7 b

07 Explain to students that they are now going to scan the text for information.

Draw students' attention to *Tip 7,* which states that in many of the IELTS reading tasks the answers appear in the same order as the text. Check students understand the meaning of this by asking: "Where in the text is the answer to Exercise 07, question 1? (beginning) 3? (middle) 6? (end).

Tell students to complete Exercise 07. Again set a time limit.

> 1 Mukesh Ambani   2 27   3 marble
> 4 the lotus flower and the sun   5 168   6 600

> **Paraphrasing**
>
> Paraphrasing is to repeat something using different words, often in a shortened form, which makes the meaning clearer.
>
> It is useful in the IELTS reading exam because many of the questions paraphrase what is written in the text. It is important therefore that candidates understand the concept of paraphrasing.

08 Ask students to read the definition of paraphrasing in the student book. Elicit from students why it may be useful for the exam.

Explain that each of the statements in Exercise 08 paraphrases one of the paragraphs in the text.

Dictate the first line of Exercise 08 -*The house has many desirable facilities…* Ask students to match this sentence with one of the paragraphs A-F.

Elicit from students how they approached this and which words helped them locate the answer quickly.

08
> 1 C   2 E   3 F   4 A   5 B   6 D

Tell students to complete questions 2-6 using the same method as the example.

Explain/ elicit from students that some of these words are synonyms, a key function of paraphrasing.

> **Definition**
>
> Synonyms: words or phrases that have the same or nearly the same meaning as another word or phrase in the same language.
> e.g. The words "small" and "little" are synonyms.

Synonyms are useful in the IELTS Reading exam because questions rarely use the same words as in the text, this would be too easy. Instead questions often feature synonyms of words from the text. It is important therefore, that students focus on synonyms when they are learning new vocabulary.

09 Ask students to complete Exercise 09.

> 1 e   2 f   3 g   4 c   5 b   6 a   7 h   8 d

10 Explain to students that having looked at some of the key skills needed for the reading exam, they are now going to focus on two of the task types (short answer questions and completing sentences).

Explain to students that the short-answer questions will be similar to those featured in Exercise 07. In the exam however, there will be a set word limit for the answers, so it is important that students read the question carefully.

Ask students to read the explanation of short answer questions and Tip 10/11 which states that the answers to these type of questions come in the same order as they appear in the text.

Tell students to complete Exercise 10.

> **Advice**
>
> Make students aware of the following: hyphenated words count as one word and spelling accuracy is important.

> 1 9/ nine   2 man-made snow   3 clean their room(s)

> **Extension**
>
> For further practice on this task type, ask students to create some of their own questions on the text and then ask their partner to find the answers.

11 Explain to students that another similar type of task they may be given in the exam is sentence completion.

This task requires candidates to complete sentences in a certain number of words. The instructions will indicate how many words/ numbers should be used in the answer.

> **Advice**
>
> Candidates will lose a mark if they write more than the number of words asked for. Numbers can be written and hyphenated words count as single words. The answers come in the same order as they appear in the text.

Ask students to read the advice section in the book, which explains that the sentences used in this type of task, paraphrase words and ideas from the text.

Tell students to complete Exercise 11. Ask several students the answer, before revealing the correct answer. If some answers given are incorrect, discuss why this is the case (i.e. not grammatically correct.)

> 1 mythical island   2 guests   3 architecture

GRAMMAR FOCUS: PRESENT SIMPLE/PRESENT CONTINUOUS

The purpose of exercises 12, 13 & 14 is to get students to notice the use of the present simple and present continuous in a text. Being aware of which tenses are being used, can help students to understand the meaning better.

12

Present continuous: an action which is not complete, happening at the time of speaking

Present simple: repeated actions, general facts, opinions

13

1 lives   2 believes   3 correct
4 clean   5 is entertaining

14

1 is working   2 am/'m renting   3 think
4 are/'re building   5 cleans

EXAM SKILLS

15 Explain to students that having practised the task type and some key exam skills, they are now going to complete an exam task on their own.

Tell students to complete the *exercise within a set time limit.*

1 (newspaper) publisher   2 Julia Morgan
3 3.5 million   4 3/ three   5 attend formal dinner(s)
6 the State of California   7 Europe   8 mother
9 15/fifteen years   10 every continent   11 zebras
12 (the) expensive maintenance

WRITING

OUTCOMES

- select key features of different types of graphs, charts and tables in order to describe them accurately
- use suitable verbs, adjectives and adverbs to describe trends in different ways
- compare different graphs or information in the same graph and write a summary of the main features.

OUTCOMES

This lesson relates to writing task 1; describing different types of graphs, charts and tables. More specifically, the lesson focuses on describing charts/graphs accurately and selecting key features. Make sure students understand the meaning of "key features" (main points).

The unit also provides a great deal of language, which can be used to describe the different trends, which may feature in any of the graphs/charts in task 1. Make sure students understand the meaning of "trend" (a general development or change in a situation).

The third outcome uses the skills/language from the first two outcomes to teach/practise how to compare information in either one or more graphs, and to write a summary of the main features.

These outcomes are all key and common requirements for writing task 1.

LEAD-IN

01 Ask students the following:

Have you had practice describing charts and graphs in your own language?

If so, when have you been required to do this?

Do you find reading/ interpreting graphs in your own language easy or difficult? Why/why not?

Having a clear understanding of how comfortable your students are with reading and interpreting graphs/charts in their own language, will help you gauge how much support is needed with this aspect of the exam task. For example, students who are not used to discussing graphs and charts will not only need support with the language, but also with the skill of interpreting this type of data.

Tell students to complete Exercise 1 on their own and then compare answers with a partner. Whole class feedback.

2 line   3 horizontal axis   4 vertical axis   5 bar chart
6 bar   7 key   8 title   9 pie chart   10 segment
11 table   12 column   13 row

Draw students' attention to the information box, which states that students must be very familiar with the language in the lead-in. Without this key vocabulary, students will be unable to complete this common task in the exam.

Extension

In order to practise this type of language further, you could describe/dictate various graphs/charts/tables to students, which they in turn must draw.

E.g. The horizontal axis indicates sales from 2005 until 2010….

02 Explain to students that they are going to practise selecting just the key features of graphs/charts.

Advice

Make students aware that they will be penalised for irrelevance or if their response is off-topic. They only have 20 minutes and 150 words for this task, so they should only report on the key features. While students won't be penalised for writing more than the word limit, they may leave themselves less time for Task 2, which is worth more marks.

Ask students which city they think is the most expensive to buy a home in.

After gathering a few ideas, tell students to look at the first chart in Exercise 02.

As a whole-class discuss questions 1-6.

1   The world's most expensive cities
2   The cost per square metre in US dollars
3   Cities

> 4 The cost per square metre in each city
> 5 shortest – Monaco tallest – New York/Singapore
> 6 Monaco, Hong Kong and London are very similar; New York and Singapore significantly more expensive

Tell students to complete questions 7-21 in pairs.

> 7 Home ownership in some European countries
> 8 Percentage of people owning their own home
> 9 some European countries
> 10 Romania has the largest percentage of homeowners and Switzerland the smallest.
> 11 Most of the countries have similar figures, except for Romania.
> 12 Romania has a much higher percentage of homeowners than the other countries.
> 13 Average house size in selected countries
> 14 Different countries
> 15 Australia/Hong Kong
> 16 Australia/USA
> 17 Average size of houses in selected European countries
> 18 Two: countries/size
> 19 Denmark
> 20 Italy
> 21 France/Germany

03 Explain to students, that reading and interpreting the charts/graphs correctly is just as important as the quality of their English. Accuracy is one of the aspects students will be marked on, under the criteria of Task Achievement.

Ask students to read the sample answer in Exercise 03 and amend any data, which is incorrect. Whole class feedback.

03
> 1 The pie chart provides information about the average house size in selected countries and the table in selected European countries.
> 2 the USA
> 3 45 m2
> 4 selected
> 5 most houses in Europe are much smaller than in the selected non-European countries
> 6 Hong Kong

04 Elicit the answer to Exercise 04.

> The writer did not make any errors with spelling or punctuation, but should not have included opinions (e.g. 'This is perhaps because it is such a large country'; 'This is most probably due to the size of each country').

Students aware that they will be penalised for giving their own opinion or speculative explanations. The answer to this task should be purely <u>factual</u>.

05 Explain to students that they are now going to practise describing trends within graphs/charts.

Draw the arrows shown in Exercise 05 on the board and elicit from students as much vocabulary as possible.

Tell students to complete Exercise 05.

> 2 Increase 3 Climb 4 Go up 5 Rocket 6 Soar
> 8 Decrease 9 Decline 10 Go down 11 Plummet
> 12 Plunge 13 Drop
> Possible other words: rise, surge, shoot up, peak, fall, reduce, collapse, tumble, diminish, sink, dip

Exercises 05-15 provide students with the necessary language needed to describe trends, exploring the use of verbs, adverbs and adjectives. Students need to make sure they know these words, how they are used and how they are spelt. In task 1, under the criterion, Lexical Resource, students are marked on their ability to use a range of vocabulary, both accurately and appropriately. At this level, at least some attempt to use less common vocabulary is also a requirement to achieve high marks.

Advice

Make students aware that they will be penalised for incorrect spelling. It is common for students to spell some of these words incorrectly, so it is useful to check students' understanding of this.

> 1 rocket, soar 2 plummet, plunge

07 Exercise 07 reminds students that when they are using these key verbs they must remember to also apply the correct tense. Draw students' attention to the example in exercise 07. Tell students to complete exercise 07.

> 1 rose 2 remains / has remained/ remainded
> 3 has decreased 4 are going to go up
> 5 have rocketed

Whole class feedback. Elicit from students which tense they used for each and why.

08
> **Big change:** dramatic, substantial, significant
> **Small change:** slight, modest
> **Gradual or no change:** steady, stable, unchanged

09
> 1 significant / substantial / dramatic
> 2 steady
> 3 slight, modest
> 4 unchanged / stable / steady

10
> 1 C 2 A 3 B

11

Big change:	dramatically, substantially
Small change:	moderately
Gradual change:	gradually, slowly, consistently
Quick change:	sharply, rapidly

12

1 significantly / considerably / substantially / dramatically
2 slightly / moderately
3 gradually / steadily / slowly / consistently
4 sharply / quickly / rapidly

13 Monitor the pair work.

14 Check students' answers for the gap-fill activity

1 B Dubai   2 C Hong Kong   3 A London

15 This exercise asks students to make a note of any new words or phrases they have learnt during the lesson. It is important that students make a habit of recording new words as having an extensive vocabulary is key to being successful in the exam.

15

1 went up, plummeted dramatically
2 remained, peak, rise
3 increased steadily, decreased substantially, went up

EXAM SKILLS

16 Explain to students that having studied all the necessary skills/vocabulary needed for this task, they are now going to complete an exam task on their own.

Tell students to complete the timed task in class or assign as homework.

Feedback

Before marking the answers yourself, you could ask students to assess what they and their partner have written. In pairs, students could discuss the positive and negative aspects of their work (self- assessment is an important learning tool for students and helps them to form the habit of self-reflection.)

Provide students with the following checklist:

Is the information accurate?

Is the information expressed clearly?

Is there a good use of tenses and vocabulary?(adjectives, adverbsetc..)

16

Sample answer

The bar chart shows how many people aged 25–34 either rent or have bought a house in the UK. Furthermore, it illustrates this change over an eleven-year period.

The number of home owners within this age range has decreased substantially since 2004. In 2004, nearly 60% owned their own home, whereas in 2014 this dropped to under 40%. There was a gradual decrease in home ownership over the eleven-year period which was more significant from 2009 to 2014. Only in 2011 and 2012 did the number remain stable at just over 40%.

The rental market, however, has increased dramatically over the same eleven-year period. From 2004 to 2014, the number of people renting has risen by nearly 30%. Again, this has been a gradual increase in most years, rising by just a few percent each year. In 2014, the rental market reached a peak at just under 50%.

In conclusion, therefore, it is easily apparent from this bar chart that for people between the ages of 25 and 34, the rental market is increasing each year, whereas the buyers' market is decreasing.

Alternative

Students could work in small groups to produce an answer to this task. They could then present their work to the class.

LISTENING

OUTCOMES

- predict the type of information required for short-answer questions
- listen for specific information (e.g. complex numbers, difficult spellings) and write it down correctly
- listen to understand context
- answer multiple-choice questions correctly by eliminating distractors.

OUTCOMES

Draw students' attention to the outcomes. This unit covers two IELTS tasks, short- answer questions and multiple-choice questions. Multiple-choice questions require students to listen carefully to have an understanding of either specific or general points. Whereas short-answer questions, require students to listen for facts such as names of places or people.

In order for students to be successful in these two tasks, several listening skills are also explored/practised in the unit. For multiple-choice questions *eliminating distractors* is a key skill which students need to be aware of.

Definition

Distractors: the incorrect options in a multiple choice question. Designed to distract students from choosing the correct answer.

Eliminating distractors therefore, is the skill of discarding the incorrect options in a multiple choice question.

For short-answer questions, the skills of prediction and listening for specific information are key. Elicit meaning from students.

LEAD-IN

01 Tell students to look at picture of the *For Sale* sign. Elicit who is usually responsible for selling houses? (an estate agent)

Tell students to look at the three properties in Exercise 1.

As a whole class, discuss the main features of Property A (e.g. flat, two levels, 3 bedrooms, a bathroom, kitchen & living room).

In pairs ask students to discuss Property B and C in the same way.

Tell students to listen to the recording and complete Exercise 01.

Tapescript 02

1 This is a very nice ground floor two-bedroom flat. It was recently modernised, with a new bathroom and kitchen. The main bedroom is a double bedroom with an en-suite bathroom and toilet, in addition to the main bathroom and toilet. There is a second, smaller bedroom. The living room is spacious and there is a large kitchen, which is big enough to be used as a dining room. The garden is accessible through the living room and the kitchen.

2 This first floor flat is in a very nice area of the town and is connected to local shops and services, as well as having good transport connections. There are two double bedrooms, one bathroom, a newly fitted kitchen, a living room and a separate dining room, which could be turned into a third bedroom. There are stairs to the garden at the back. The flat needs some modernisation, but it is very well-kept and would be an excellent family home.

3 This is a lovely flat, suitable for a family or for people sharing. The flat is on two levels – there's a first floor and a second floor, above a separate ground floor flat. Upstairs, there's a large double bedroom and a smaller double, as well as a third bedroom, which is only a single, but is still a good size. There's a large bathroom upstairs and also a small shower room downstairs. There's a spacious living room and a large kitchen/dining room, with a rear door to steps leading to the garden.

1 C	2 B	3 A

Advice

This type of multiple-choice task is common in the exam and students must have practice in being able to interpret pictures/diagrams quickly. They need to identify the key features in these visuals and then listen for the same key information in the recording.

02 Tell students to listen again and note down the key words, which helped them locate the correct answer.

02
1 ground floor, two bedroom
2 first floor, two double bedrooms, one bathroom
3 two levels, large double bedroom, smaller double, third bedroom spacious livingroom,large kitchen, diningroom

Ask students to compare their notes with a partner. Whole class feedback-did they choose the same information?

03 Tell students to look at the notes in *Exercise 3*. Elicit from students what type of information is missing from each gap? Also, ask for examples, e.g. address of property - 33, Whitehill Road.

Explain to students that this type of prediction is a very useful exam technique, as it helps students to focus on the type of language required, even before listening to the recording.

Draw students' attention to *Tip 3*, stating that students will be given the context and some time to look at the questions before they start. Students should use this time therefore, to underline key words and carry out this type of prediction technique.

Tell students to listen to the recording and complete the notes with no more than two words/or a number.

Advice

Make students aware that if they write more than the stated number of words, it will be marked as incorrect, so they should read the question very carefully. Hyphenated words count as single words.

Tapescript 03

Estate agent:	Morgan's Estate Agents. How can I help you?
Caroline:	Hello. I'm calling about a property that you have for sale – in Churchill Road.
Estate agent:	Sorry. Did you say Church Mill Road?
Caroline:	No. Churchill Road – C-H-U-R-C-H-I-L-L.
Estate agent:	Oh, right. We have two for sale in Churchill Road – a three-bedroom property and a two-bedroom one. Can you tell me which one you're calling about?
Caroline:	It's the three-bedroom one.
Estate agent:	Oh, yes. Would you like to arrange a viewing?
Caroline:	Yes, but first of all, I'd like to check some details.
Estate agent:	Certainly. What would you like to know?
Caroline:	First how many lounges has it got?
Estate agent:	There are two. There's a small one at the front and a larger one at the back, leading to a sun-room.
Caroline:	A sun room? That's nice to know.
Estate agent:	Yes. It's perfect to sit in on those chilly or rainy days as it's got its own heating. And you can get to the garden through the sun-room door.
Caroline:	Lovely. I've always liked the idea of outdoor space with a lawn. I do a bit of gardening myself. What about the kitchen?
Estate agent:	It's fully-fitted – so it includes a cooker and a dishwasher and all the other things you'd expect in a kitchen. You can also get to the outside space through the kitchen door.
Caroline:	That sounds great, not having to buy a cooker and dishwasher.
Estate agent:	Yes, it would be perfect for you. I should add that there's a garage and a short driveway.
Caroline:	Oh, that's very useful. My husband usually drives to work, but I mostly use public transport.
Estate agent:	Well, regarding transport, it's only five minutes from Edgely Station and there are regular buses to the town centre, so it's very well connected.
Caroline:	That's excellent!
Estate agent:	So, would you like to arrange a viewing?
Caroline:	I'm free tomorrow morning. Is 11 o'clock OK?

Estate agent:	Oh, no, I'm sorry. I'm busy then.
Caroline:	How about one o'clock then, or one forty-five?
Estate agent:	One o'clock would be best for me.
Caroline:	OK, great. Let's meet then. Oh, my name is Caroline Prendergast. My number is 07945 872310.
Estate agent:	I'm Peter Eliot.
Caroline:	Is that with two 'l's?
Estate agent:	No, one: E-L-I-O-T. My number is 07863 905073. That's 07863 905073. I look forward to seeing you then.
Caroline:	OK. Goodbye.
Estate agent:	Goodbye.

1	Churchill Road	2	Three / 3	3	Two / 2
4	garden	5/6	(a) cooker	6/5	(a) dishwasher
7	1 / one o'clock	8	Eliot	9	07863905073

04 Exercises 04 and 05 practise students' ability to understand and write down numbers. This is a common requirement of the exam, and therefore students must feel confident in this area. It is advisable that students write down numbers as figures rather than words, in order to avoid any errors in spelling.

Tell students to listen to the short conversations in *Exercise 04* and complete questions 1-5.

Tapescript 04
Conversation 1

A:	How much is that altogether?
B:	That's £53.72, please.
A:	Sorry, did you say £43.72?
B:	No, £53.72.

Conversation 2

A:	So how far is it to Paris?
B:	I've just checked. It's 472 km.
A:	472 km? That's a long way. Are you sure you want to drive?

Conversation 3

A:	Someone left a message for you, Mr Henry. He wants you to call him on 01897 625730.
B:	Sorry, I didn't get all that. Did you say 01857 629730?
A:	No, it's 01897 625730.

Conversation 4

A:	So how big is the football field?
B:	It's 110 m by 55 m.
A:	110 m long and 55 m wide? That's quite big.

Conversation 5

A:	Can I book a place on the course on Saturday, please?
B:	Certainly madam. What's your membership number?
A:	It's B1074.
B:	Sorry, did you say D1074?

A:	No, B1074.
B:	Oh, OK, thank you.

1	£53.72	2	472 km
3	01897 625730	4	110 m x 55 m 5 B1074

05 In Exercise 05 students are presented with more complex numbers. Tell students to complete exercise 05. It may be useful to remind candidates that they are only listening for numbers here, as the measurement is already included (m)

Tapescript 05

Estate agent:	Hello. I'm Peter Eliot. You must be Ms Prendergast?
Caroline:	Yes, that's right.
Estate agent:	So, this is the property.
Caroline:	Oh, I just wanted to check one thing – the price. If I remember rightly, it's £340,000?
Estate agent:	Actually, it's £350,000 at the moment, but we can discuss that later if you like it. As you can see, the front garden is very well kept.
Caroline:	Yes. The owners have taken very good care of it.
Estate agent:	Shall we go in? Follow me Here's the hall and the front lounge to the left.
Caroline:	Hmm, yes. It's very nice. What are the dimensions?
Estate agent:	It's 4.3 m by 3.28 m. That's very spacious for a smaller lounge.
Caroline:	Hmm, yes. 4.3 m long and 3.28 m wide. Can we go through to the second lounge?
Estate agent:	Certainly. If you'd like to follow me.
Caroline:	Ooh, it's lovely. What's the size of this room?
Estate agent:	Er, let's see … the second lounge … er … it's 6.5 m x 4.25 m. And you can see the sun-room at the back and the garden.
Caroline:	Can we go and have a look?
Estate agent:	Of course. As you can see, there's enough room here for some plants and two sofas. You could even put a dining suite here.
Caroline:	That would be perfect for cooler days. I love it!
Estate agent:	And as you can see, there's a patio and a large lawn with flowers round the edges.
Caroline:	What are the dimensions of the garden?
Estate agent:	It's 30 m long and 10 m wide.
Caroline:	30 m by 10 m? That's a good size for a family. It would be lovely in summer.
Estate agent:	Of course. Walk this way. Would you like to look upstairs?
Caroline:	Yes, OK.
Estate agent:	Here's the main bedroom. It's 4.91 m x 3.95 m – perfect for a large double bed. Oh, sorry, that's 4.91 m long and 3.95 m wide.

	And there's an en-suite bathroom here, though it only has a shower unit and not a big bath like the main bathroom.
Caroline:	That would come in very useful when we all get up to get ready for school or work.
Estate agent:	Yes, that's a real positive. Here's the second bedroom. It's 4.2 m x 3.55 m – ideal for children to share.
Caroline:	4.2 m long and 3.55 m wide? OK, that's good. Yes, it's got plenty of room to play in.
Estate agent:	And here's the last bedroom which is 3.25 m x 2.5 m. It would be ideal for a child.
Caroline:	Yes, it would be fine for my older daughter.
Estate agent:	The bathroom is just over here. It's got a large bath as well as a shower fitting.
Caroline:	Great! It's just what we need.
Estate agent:	So, would you like to put in an offer?
Caroline:	Yes, please. This is the best property I've seen so far. I don't think I'll find a more suitable one.
Estate agent:	Wonderful! If you'd like to come back to the office, I can take your details and arrange everything.

05

1 £350,000	2 4.3 x 3.28 m	3 30 x 10 m
4 4.91 x 3.95 m	5 4.2 x 3.55 m	

Extension

If you feel that your students need more practice with understanding and writing down numbers you could try the following exercise.

Divide the class into pairs and ask each student to write down ten numbers, without showing their partner (make sure students write down a variety of fairly complex numbers) One student then dictates their numbers, whilst the other writes them down. The roles are then reversed.

06 Tell students they are going to listen to the final conversation between the estate agent and client.

Ask students to read through the questions in Exercise 06 carefully, and predict the type of information required for each.

Tapescript 06

Estate agent:	So, Ms Prendergast, let me take your details. I'll just enter your name. How do you spell it?
Caroline:	P-R-E-N-D-E-R-G-A-S-T.
Estate agent:	OK, that's it. And what's your present address?
Caroline:	52, Lanchester Road. That's L-A-N-C-H-E-S-T-E-R. It's in the Riverside part of town. The postcode is KE7 8UD.
Estate agent:	And your home phone number?
Caroline:	01594 398210.
Estate agent:	And I've got your mobile number: 07945 872310.
Caroline:	Yes, that's right.
Estate agent:	OK. Now the house is on the market for £350,000, but I know that the owners would be happy to accept a close offer as it's been on for a few months. What would your first offer be?
Caroline:	I think £340,000 would be fair.
Estate agent:	OK. I'll put that offer to them and we'll see what they say. Now, usually buyers have a mortgage arranged with a bank – a loan to buy the house, so that we can quickly complete the sale. Do you have one arranged yet?
Caroline:	We've spoken to our bank and they're happy to offer us what we need, up to £300,000. We also have a 15% deposit in our bank account – about £52,000 – so that won't be a problem.
Estate agent:	And is anyone buying your house? Will the sellers of this property need to wait for you to sell yours?
Caroline:	No. We sold it a couple of months ago and we're staying with relatives, so we're ready to move in as soon as the sale is completed. So, when do you think you can get an answer on the offer?
Estate agent:	I should be able to get one tomorrow. Then, if they agree, we can do things quite quickly. Your bank will do the survey – you know, send someone to check the house is in good condition and at the right price, and, if that's OK, we can then prepare the contracts for you and the seller to sign.
Caroline:	How long do you think the sale will take after that?
Estate agent:	Well, it's difficult to say. If things go well, we should complete it in about two months at the most. Most sales take about two months. However, if there are any problems, it could take longer, but we hope it won't be more than three months. For example, part of the house, like the roof, might be in bad condition and might need some work. Or there might be plans for a new road in the local area. Anything like that can delay the sale, but most of our sales go through quickly.
Caroline:	Oh, I hope nothing like that happens! We're really looking forward to moving in soon. It's not easy living a long time with relatives, and my husband has a long journey to get to work, but those aren't the things I'm really worried about. If we can move in before the end of the summer, it'll

be much easier for the children to go to their new school. That's why I hope we can complete everything on time.

Estate agent: Don't worry. I don't see any problems with this sale, so I'm quite sure you'll be in the house by then. So, just to go over things again: I'll talk to the sellers tomorrow. If they accept your offer, then we can continue. If they don't, you'll need to put in a higher one quickly, but we should be able to agree by the end of the week. Then you ask your bank to send someone to check the house. If that's all OK, the next step is to prepare the contracts for you and the seller to sign, and we should complete the sale soon after that.

Caroline: Wonderful! I'll look forward to your call tomorrow. Bye.

Estate agent: Bye.

06
1 name, address and home phone number
2 mortgage from bank and deposit in bank account
3 two months (three at the most)
4 C (she wants to move in before her children start school)

07 Explain to students that in order to test their full understanding of the listening, the multiple choice questions will feature incorrect answers which may seem correct. These are called 'distractors.'

In order to give them an example of this, ask students to read Exercise 07 and play part of the recording again.

Tapescript 07

Estate agent: And there's an en-suite bathroom here, though it only has a shower unit and not a big bath like the main bathroom.

Caroline: That would come in very useful when we all get up to get ready for school or work.

Ask students which is the correct answer? (C) Also, ask students which answer is not correct, but is true? (A) Which option is not true or correct? (B)

Explain to students that some answers may be true therefore, but not correct and this is a type of distraction. Another form of distraction is mentioning something in the negative, 'not a big bath like the main bathroom.'

Advice

Students must always listen carefully for little words such as 'not' which can change the whole meaning of a sentence or phrase.

EXAM SKILLS

08 Explain to students that they are now going to do some exam practice. Before doing so, ask students to read *Tip 8* carefully. Like the reading exam, the recordings in the listening will use synonyms of the words in the question. Refer students to the tapescript 06.

---

1 B	2 C	3 A	4 B	5 A

SPEAKING

OUTCOMES

- speak about various aspects of where you live for Speaking Part 1
- respond to wh-,would and Yes/No questions about where you live
- prepare more information for common Speaking Part 1 topics
- use syllable stress in words correctly.

OUTCOMES

This unit prepares students for Part 1 of the speaking test, which focuses on students' ability to speak about everyday topics, by answering a selection of questions. Outcome 1 deals with a very common topic in this part, speaking about where you live.

This unit also aims to enhance students' pronunciation in general, by focusing on syllable stress in words.

Definition
Syllable stress: the part of the word you give most emphasis to.

LEAD-IN

01 Tell students to briefly discuss in pairs what they like/dislike about their home town, e.g.
There are lots of shops / There aren't enough shops.

If needed, you could start by giving your own example of what you like/dislike about your hometown.

Tell students to look at the vocabulary list in Exercise 01 and decide which column in the table each word belongs to. Again, students should discuss their choices in pairs.

02 Tell students they are now going to listen to an extract from Speaking Part 1. They must listen carefully and answer the questions in Exercise 02.

Tapescript 08

Examiner: Now, in this section of the test, I'd like to ask you some questions about yourself and where you live. Do you live in a house or an apartment at the moment?

Student: Right now, I'm living in a house with two other students. It's a pretty big house with two floors, a garden and a shared bathroom. I moved in during the summer.

Examiner: Where do you live – in the city or the countryside?

Student: Our house is in the city centre, about five minutes' walk from the train station. We're close to all of the shops and restaurants, and our school is about a 20 minutes' bus ride from my house. There's lots to see and do around there, so I'm pretty happy with the location.

Examiner: Who else lives with you where you live?

Student: Well, as I said – I live with two other students – they both go to the same school as me. One of them is from China and the other is from India. I'm from Romania, so I think we live in a pretty international house!

Examiner: Is there anything you don't like about where you live?

Student: Well, I don't like sharing my bathroom with others and the kitchen is often very busy, but I think that's normal for a shared house. Also, we need to do the gardening regularly or things get out of control. Sometimes the trains can be a little loud as well, especially in the mornings.

Examiner: Now, let's talk about shopping. Where do most people go shopping where you live?

Student: Most people go to the Citygate shopping centre, as it's the biggest and has the most shops and restaurants. There's also a cinema and ice-rink, so people go there not just to shop, but to hang out with their friends as well. It has all of the famous brands and most importantly, it's warm in the winter!

Examiner: When do you usually go shopping?

Student: I usually go at the weekends as I'm too busy with my studies to go in the week. The only problem is that the Citygate gets very full at weekends and you have to wait a long time to get a bus back home, because so many people are trying to catch the bus at the same time as you.

Examiner: Why do lots of young people like to go shopping at big shopping centres?

Student: I think it's because everything is in one place, and they're clean and comfortable and safe for young people to meet. Where else can you go that has all of the shops and entertainment under one roof that the big malls have?

Examiner: Would you ever do your shopping at the local market?

Student: I'm not really sure as the local market is more for older people who just want to go and buy some cheaper food or clothes, and the styles and brands on sale at the market are a bit old-fashioned for me, personally. Maybe my parents would be fine with going to the market, but there's really nothing interesting for me there.

02

1 8 questions.

2 *Wh-* questions – *Where, Who, When, Why; Would* questions; *Yes/No* questions with *Is* and *Do*

3 where (you) live; shopping

4 Approximately 15–20 seconds; 3–4 sentences per question

Draw students' attention to Tip 2, stating that the *Why* question usually comes last and might be more difficult to answer.

Advice

Tell students not to spend too long thinking about the most truthful answer. The examiner is testing their level of English, nothing else. The notion of inventing ideas can prove difficult for some students, so practice may be needed in this area.

03 Explain to students that most of the Speaking Part 1 questions are Wh- questions. Elicit these from students (What? Who? When? and Why?)

Tell students that they are going to listen to the same recording again and that they should note down any language the student uses to describe their home and shopping facilities.

Home: pretty big house, two floors, garden, shared bathroom, city centre, about five minutes' walk, about twenty minutes' bus ride, I'm (pretty) happy with the location, Well, I don't like, shared house, the trains can be a little loud

Shopping: shopping centre, cinema, ice-rink, hang out, famous brands, gets very full, everything is in one place, clean and comfortable, entertainment, under one roof, local market, styles and brands, old-fashioned.

04 Exercises 04 & 05 practise some of the questions students may be asked in Part 1.

Tell them to ask/answer these questions in pairs.

Monitor students carefully, with the following marking criteria in mind: fluency/coherence, lexical resource, grammatical range and accuracy & pronunciation.

At this level, it may be more appropriate to just correct errors relating to one or two of these areas, depending on the strength/weaknesses of your particular students.

Advice

In Part 1 students shouldn't just answer *yes* or *no* or expand too much i.e. go off topic and start talking about something else.

Feedback

Instead of correcting errors as you hear them and interrupting students in mid flow, you could make a note of some of the most common errors and present them to the entire class at the end of the activity.

06 Draw students' attention to the information section which states that there are a number of possible topics students might be asked in Speaking Part 1, such as news, entertainment or sport.

Tell students to complete Exercise 06.

07 Questions 7 & 8 deal with Yes/No questions, another common feature of Part 1.

Questions which usually start with Do(es) or Is?/Are?.

Draw students' attention to *Tip 7,* stating that students shouldn't just answer Yes or No, but should also add at least two sentences explaining their answer. Exercise 07 provides examples of this.

Tell students to complete Exercise 07.

1 b	2 d	3 a	4 f	5 c	6 e

Tell students to complete Exercise 08 and monitor the length and relevancy of their answers.

09 Explain to students that sometimes there are many different ways to express the same type of question.

Tell them to read the example related to "weather".

Write the word "restaurants" on the board in a bubble. Elicit from students four different questions associated with this topic.

How often do you go to a restaurant? What is your favourite restaurant etc.?

Tell students to complete the rest of the bubbles in Exercise 09.

Tell students to ask and answer the questions in pairs.

10 Tell students to add two more topics to the mindmap and again create four questions for each.

Sample answer
Other topics: sport, healthcare

Syllable Stress

Explain to students that in the speaking exam they also need to focus on their pronunciation. Using the correct syllable stress is just one aspect which will make sure they are clearly understood.

Write the following sentence on the board:

Right now, I am living in an apartment with my friends.

Ask students, to underline the stress in the word *apartment* and then check the answer in Exercise 11.

11 Tell students they are going to listen to these 16 words (Exercise 11) in the recording and they have to underline the stressed syllable in each.

Tapescript 09

1   Right now I'm living in an apartment with my friends.
2   I'm not too happy with my current accommodation – it's too small.
3   The architecture in my home town is fascinating.
4   I get up early as there's a lot of construction going on across the road.
5   My shopping mall has a lot of escalators, as there are ten floors in total.
6   The inhabitants of my home town are pretty easy-going as we live in a place with good weather.
7   The most famous monument in my home town is the Statue of Liberty.
8   Most visitors to my home town go to the museum as it's very famous.
9   The most boring places in my home town are the residential areas, as there are no shops there.
10 My home town has a huge stadium where people go to see the local football team.
11 These days, many people are leaving the city to go to the countryside, where it's cleaner.

12 I'd say that due to the traffic in my home town, the environment there is getting worse.
13 My home town has an interesting geography with big mountains and deep valleys.
14 The most interesting thing about where I live is the regional food that you can only get here.
15 On average we get pretty warm temperatures here in my home town.
16 Because I live in the countryside, the scenery here is beautiful – very colourful and bright.

2 ac / com / o / <u>da</u> / tion   3 ar /chi/ tec/ ture
4 con/<u>struc</u> / tion   5 es / ca/ la /tor   6 in / <u>ha</u> / bi /tants
7 <u>mon</u> / u / ment   8 mu /<u>se</u> /um   9 res/ i/ <u>den</u>/ tial
10 <u>sta</u> / di / um   11 <u>coun</u> / try / side   12 en /<u>vi</u> / ron /ment
13 ge /<u>og</u>/ ra/phy   14 <u>re</u> /gion /al   15 <u>temp</u> /er /a / ture
16 <u>sce</u> /ne/ry

12 Tell students to listen to the words again and repeat them with the correct syllable stress.

Tapescript 10

1   A / <u>part</u> / ment   2   Ac / com / o / <u>da</u> / tion
3   <u>Ar</u> /chi/ tec/ ture   4   Con/<u>struc</u> / tion   5   <u>Es</u> / ca/ la /tors
6   In / <u>ha</u> / bi /tants   7   <u>Mon</u> / u / ment   8   Mu /<u>se</u>/um
9   Res/ i/ <u>den</u>/ tial   10   <u>Sta</u> / di / um   11   <u>Coun</u> / try / side
12   En /<u>vi</u> / ron /ment   13   Ge /<u>og</u>/ ra/phy   14   <u>Re</u> /gion /al
15   <u>Temp</u> /er /a / tures   16   <u>Sce</u> /ne/ry

EXAM SKILLS

13 Tell students to complete *this exercise* in pairs. Without interrupting to correct errors, monitor students carefully and assess which areas they need more help with before the exam. i.e. lexical, pronunciation.

This exercise stipulates three sentences, as students need to be careful about the length of their answers. Answers should not be too long or too short, and therefore asking candidates to produce three sentences demonstrates roughly how long they should speak for.

UNIT / 02: LEISURE AND RECREATION

READING

> ### OUTCOMES
>
> - identify questions which ask for factual information and questions which ask for the writer's opinion
> - skim and scan to arrive at the correct answers quickly
> - understand the whole text to answer questions about global understanding
> - use the past simple and past continuous correctly.

OUTCOMES

The outcomes of this lesson focus mainly on the skills needed to complete multiple-choice questions. These include understanding the text as a whole, skimming/scanning and identifying questions as either factual or as the writer's opinion.

LEAD-IN

01 Elicit from students what their favourite sport is and who their favourite sports personality is.

Ask students to complete Exercises 01, 02 & 03. These exercises aim to engage students in the topic of *sport*, a common theme in the exam.

01

> 1 Muhammad Ali   2 Michael Jordan   3 Serena Williams
> 4 David Beckham   5 Jack Nicklaus

02

> 1 Boxing   2 Basketball   3 Tennis   4 Football   5 Golf

03 Draw students' attention to the information box, stating that although the IELTS Reading will feature multiple-choice questions, as in Exercise 03, they will not test students' general knowledge. All the answers will be in the text provided.

> 1 B   2 A   3 B   4 C   5 A

04 Make students aware that there are two types of question in the reading exam: questions, which ask for factual information and questions, which ask for the writer's opinion.

Tell students to read the paragraphs about Muhammad Ali and answer the questions. Draw students' attention to *Tip 4*, stating that the answers are in the same order as the text.

> 1 B   2 B

05 Tell students to complete Exercise 05.

> 1 1: opinion 2: factual
> 2 yes, most appropriate answer chosen
> 3 yes, *appeal*, *successful athlete*, no, matching words are often misleading
> 4 *referred to himself*

Advice

At this level it is important that students are able to understand the writer's opinion. The opinion of the writer might not always be given directly and students will have to analyse the language used carefully, to understand the view being expressed.

> ### Sample answer
>
> *I think Muhammed Ali is a legend because of several factors not just his abilities as a boxer. (This view is directly expressed, which is unlikely in the exam.)*
> *There is much more to this man's appeal. Not only is he a successful athlete, but he is also known for his strong work ethic and fearless approach to standing up for his beliefs. (This view is less direct and more common in the exam.)*

Extension

Write the following sentences on the board and ask students to match to one of the following: surprised, grateful, excited, disappointed or optimistic.

1. I can't wait until the Final!
2. I am just so happy to be a part of this amazing competition.
3. It was ok, I have had better matches.
4. Tomorrow should go well, I am in good physical shape.
5. I can't believe my horse won, it certainly wasn't the favourite to win.

06 Draw students' attention to the information box, which states that due to the length of texts in the exam, candidates need to develop a strategy, which will allow them to access the correct answers quickly.

Tell students to complete Exercise 06.

> 1 questions, instructions   3 key   4 Scan   5 wrong

07 Tell students to use the approach in Exercise 06 to complete Exercise 07. Make them aware of *Tip 7*, stating that the number of letters you need to choose can vary.

> 1 B, D 2 B, C 3 A,B

08 Tell students to complete Exercise 08 and draw their attention to *Tip 8 which points out* that some questions require you to answer the question and others to complete the sentence.

> 1 Complete: 1, 3 Question: 2

> 1 Text: *powerful*, Question: *strong*; Text: *determination*, Question: *self-belief*
> 2 Text: *be important*, Question: *focused on*; Text: *training to be*, *tennis stars* Question: *tennis training*; Text: *education*, Question: *studies*
> 3 Text: *speed of thought*, Question: *thinks quickly*; Text: *powerful shots*, Question: *can hit the ball hard*

03

> 1 Answers: *fashion*, Text: *fashion*
> 2 Answers: *home*, Text: *home*; Answers: *training*, Text: *training*; Answers: *star*, Text: *star*
> 3 Answers: *hit*, Text: *hit*; Answers: *third fastest*, Text: *third fastest*; Answers: *opponents*, Text: *opponents*

04

> In questions 1 and 2, no, the same words are not used in the text and the correct answers. In question 3, both the text and one of the correct answers use the word *hit*.

GRAMMAR FOCUS: PAST SIMPLE / PAST CONTINUOUS

09–13 The purpose of exercises 09–13 is to get students to recognise the meaning and use of the past simple/continuous.

09

> past simple, past continuous, present perfect

10

> 1 she was playing …, Serena hit …
> 2 playing a match / hitting a serve
> 3 Long, continued action: playing a match; short, finished action: hit a serve
> 4 yes

11

> 1 whilst they were training
> 2 past continuous, past simple

12

> 1 was playing, rang
> 2 fell, (he was) running
> 3 started
> 4 was raining

13

> **Sample answers**
>
> a he threw the ball to his opponent   b he was scoring a goal   c he heard a loud noise

14 This section will practise students' ability to gain an understanding of a text as a whole. Draw students' attention to *Tip 14*, stating that the answer to this question type will not be based just on one or two paragraphs but on the whole text.

Advice

Reading the whole text can be time-consuming, so make sure students are skimming the text and underlining key words. Writing notes to summarise each paragraph can also help.

Tell students to complete Exercise 14.

Extension

For further practice with this type of question, give students a selection of texts/articles and ask them to think of the most appropriate title.

B

EXAM SKILLS

15 Set a time limit and tell students to complete the practice exam task. Remind students that answers come in the same order as the text.

> 1 B   2 C   3 B   4 B

Extension

In order to give more students practice with multiple-choice questions, you could try the following:

ask your class what sports they are interested in

find articles related to that topic

ask the students to think of multiple-choice questions in pairs/small groups for their article

students swap their articles and answer the questions

WRITING

> **OUTCOMES**
>
> - select and compare key features of charts, graphs and tables
> - structure an answer which compares information from charts, graphs and tables
> - revise the form and use of comparatives.

OUTCOMES

This unit focuses on Part 1 of the written exam. All three outcomes aim to help students compare the main features in charts, graphs and tables. Students may be asked to write about more than one graph/chart in this Part and therefore it is important that they are able to select the key features in each.

The second outcome helps students to compare the information presented by two graphs/charts. This is also supported by a revision of comparatives, a key component when making comparisons.

Thirdly, this unit focuses on structuring this type of answer. Structure is very important here, as potentially, there is a great deal to write about in this task type. Candidates must learn to order their ideas clearly, therefore, in order to produce the most comprehensive answer possible.

LEAD-IN

01 Write the words *Summer Olympics* and *Winter Olympics* on the board. Elicit and feed sports which may feature in each.

athletics   skiing

Summer Olympics   Winter Olympics

swimming   ice-skating

This will engage students in the topic and practise/boost students' vocabulary for the exam.

Tell students to discuss the questions in Exercise 01.

02 Tell students to study the key features in these two graphs and then answer questions 1-3.

> **Advice**
>
> It is quite possible that students will be given more than one graph to discuss in Part 1 of the writing. Students sometimes worry about this, so they need to practise and ask themselves the following:
>
> What are the graphs about? (Look at the titles.)
>
> What types of graph/chart are they? (line, bar, pie etc.)
>
> What do they show? (Look at the titles of both axes.)
>
> What is the general trend in both? (Look at the highest and lowest points in each)
>
> What is the main difference between the data in each graph?

> 1 USA, USSR & Germany 2 Norway 3 France

03-08 Exercises 03-08 show students how to structure the answer to this type of task.

Structure (coherence & cohesion) is one of the criteria, which examiners use to assess Writing Task 1. At this level, examiners are looking for answers, which are logically organised and demonstrate a clear progression throughout.

Tell students to read the answer in Exercise 03, which illustrates clearly an example of a structured essay. Tell students to complete Exercise 04.

04
> 1 Introduction 2 Main body 3 Main body 4 Summary

Tell students to complete exercises 05-08. Draw their attention to *Tip 6,* stating that sentences should be simple and easy to understand, not long and complicated.

> **Advice**
>
> Many students believe that in order to achieve a high score, their sentences must be complex. The most important factor however, is that the meaning is clearly understood.

05
> 1 yes 2 separate 3 both

06
> 1 introduction 2 main body 3 summary

08
> 1 C 2 A 3 D 4 B

GRAMMAR FOCUS: COMPARATIVES

09-13 Exercises 09-13 aim to consolidate students' knowledge of comparative forms in order that they are confident with these structures when have to compare information in the exam. At this level, students are expected to have a good command of structures such as these, and make very few errors.

Exercises 11 & 12 also include modifiers (e.g. significantly), which will help students gain marks under the criteria of *Lexical Resource.* At this level, students are expected to demonstrate an adequate/sufficient range of vocabulary and use some less common vocabulary. For example, they should be using adverbs, as well as adjectives, to describe trends, in order to gain the band they are aiming at.

09
> 1 (significantly) more successful than

10
> achieved far more gold medals, slightly more silver and bronze medals, a little more successful than Great Britain, the same number of medals

11
> 1 slower / more slowly 2 further / farther
> 3 colder; more successful 4 more interesting
> 5 better 6 more often 7 older 8 more gracefully

12
> easily (apparent), far (more), slightly (more), a little (more)

13 Exercise 13 focuses on choosing the key and relevant information. Make students aware that this is an important requirement of Writing Part 1 and is marked under the assessment criteria of *Task achievement.* At this level, students need to be able to present a clear overview of the graphs/charts, focusing only on the main trends/differences and only reporting on appropriate information. This overview should only be a few lines long and provide a general summary of the information presented in both graphs/charts.

Tell student to complete Exercise 13.

> 1, 2, 5
> 3 and 4 just describe facts taken directly from the table (i.e. no interpretation has taken place).

Draw students' attention to *Tip 13/14,* stating that it is a good idea to group information. Elicit/ give students an example of this. Tell students to complete Exercise 14.

> 1 The most successful country is the USA, which has won over 2, 500 medals.
> 2 The line graph shows that Germany and Great Britain have won a similar number of medals.
> 3 The second most successful country is the USSR, which has won less than half the medals of the USA.

EXAM SKILLS

15 Tell students that they are now going to complete a timed exam task, using the language/skills they have acquired during the lesson.

Tell students they will be marked on the following:

The structure of their essay- Is it clear? Does it have a logical progression?

Their use of comparative structures

Their ability to choose the most relevant points/trends

Their range and use of vocabulary

You could also elicit from students some of the aspects needed to achieve the criteria above

e.g. Structure- introduction, main body overview.

Sample answer

The two charts give information about the gender and number of athletes who have entered the Games since they started. The bar chart illustrates the number of men and women entering the Games, whereas the line graph shows the number of participants.

It is evident from the bar chart that, until 2012, there were always significantly more men entering the Games than women. In 1924 and 1952, there were hardly any women entering the Games, yet in 1952 there were over 4,000 male participants. In 2012, however, the number of female athletes rose significantly to nearly 5,000, only approximately 1,000 lower than male participants.

The line graph shows a similar trend, with the number of participants increasing throughout the century. The most significant increase occurred between 1984 and 2012, when the number of athletes rose from just over 6,000 to over 10,000 in 2012.

To summarise therefore, since 1924 the number of athletes entering the Olympic Games, has increased dramatically. This is particularly the case for women, who are now represented in nearly the same numbers as male participants.

LISTENING

OUTCOMES

- listen to and understand directions from one place to another
- match descriptions with people, places or things
- listen for specific information and classify it in a table.

OUTCOMES

Draw students' attention to the outcomes of the unit, which cover three of the task types they may encounter in the exam: labelling a map, matching and table completion.

In order to complete the first task type successfully, students will need to have a good knowledge of vocabulary associated with giving directions. For the other two outcomes, it is important that candidates can identify the key words in the recording. For the table completion task, they are also required to listen for specific information. All of these skills will be discussed/ practised fully in this unit.

LEAD-IN

In order to engage students in the topic of maps/directions, draw their attention to the picture of the signpost. Elicit from students landmarks you may find in each of these places.

Suburbs: (an area where people live outside the centre of a city): school, houses, park, church etc..

Countryside: farm, fields, houses, parks

Inner city: high-rise flats, the tube, shopping centres, office blocks

Seaside: the beach, sea, restaurants, tourist office

Students could be presented with a map of one of these areas and this will help them to predict the type of language they could hear in the recording.

Extension

In pairs students could discuss which area they would prefer to live in and why.

01 Tell students to match the words in the box with the pictures below. This is very useful vocabulary and may well feature in a map completion task. This could be done in pairs or as a whole class. Depending on the level of your class, you may also need to drill whole-class the pronunciation of these words.

| 1 crossroads | 2 junction | 3 bend |
| 4 flyover | 5 traffic lights | 6 roundabout |

02 Tell students to read questions 1-6 and check they understand all the vocabulary.

Students listen to the directions and match with the correct word.

Tapescript 11

1 Stay in the middle lane so that you can go over the motorway.
2 You'll have to wait on the right till it changes for you to turn.
3 Go round and take the third exit on the right.
4 Slow down here because it goes to the left quite sharply.
5 When you get there, go straight across.
6 When you get to the end of this road, take the left turn.

| 1 flyover | 2 traffic lights | 3 roundabout |
| 4 bend | 5 crossroads | 6 junction |

03 Draw students' attention to the information box, stating that when candidates are asked to do a map completion task, it is important that they study the map given carefully, beforehand. Also, students should listen for the key information in the recording i.e direction words- turn left, straight ahead etc.

Tell students to look at the map in Exercise 03 in pairs, and discuss/ predict the kind of language they might hear in the recording.

Sample answers

petrol station, left, right, bend, straight on, roundabout, take, go etc.

Tell students to listen to the recording and write the letters A-F in the correct place on the map.

Tapescript 12

Jeff: Hi. This is Jeff here. I'm calling you all about the inter-college sports competition at the South Hinton sports centre next week. I'm really sorry but there's been a change of plan. We can't have the competition at the centre because of the flooding last week after all the rain. It damaged a lot of our equipment and also the floors in some of the rooms. Luckily, I contacted the North Hinton Sports Centre and they've kindly agreed to let us use their centre and their equipment for the competition, so I'm phoning to give you directions on how to get there and instructions about what to do there to prepare. You'll need to meet the others there next Tuesday at about nine o'clock to get the centre ready.

OK, as I'm not sure if you know how to get to North Hinton, I'll give you directions avoiding the town centre, because it can be quite busy in the morning. First, come out of our sports centre into Lily Road. Turn left and go about two hundred metres and you come to a roundabout. You see a sign to Hinton saying turn left, but that takes you into the centre of town, so don't take that one. Go straight over that roundabout and you come to a crossroads. The left turn here also takes you into the centre, so don't take that one either. Carry on for about a kilometre. The road goes up onto a flyover over the motorway to Longchester. After the flyover, you come to the junction with Bramley Road. This is where you go left, because that takes you round the town to the sports centre. Carry on for about five hundred metres. Then you go left round a bend and just after the bend you see a petrol station on the left. The turning for Hinton is just after that at the traffic lights, so make sure you look out for it. Turn right into West Road and carry on. The sports centre is on Green Lane, which is just past the Woodland Hotel on the right. You can't miss it. There's a car park there so you shouldn't have a problem parking. Please don't be late as we have a lot to do.

03

FPO

04 Tell students they are now going to focus on another type of task which features in the listening exam: matching descriptions to people, places or things. Draw students'

attention to the information box, which again reminds students to listen out for key words.

Before listening to the recording in Exercise 04, ask students to predict the key words they might hear in relation to each of these sports.

This technique is very useful for the exam, as it gives candidates a head start before they listen to the recording.

Tapescript 13

1 This game is similar to tennis, but you don't need to have such strong arms to play it; the playing area is smaller and people hit a shuttlecock – a light object with feathers – instead of a ball. You need to think and move quickly.

2 You have to be very strong in your arms and legs but also light and flexible to do this sport because you use your whole body all the time.

3 You don't need to move around a lot in this sport, but you need to think very fast and move your arms quickly and accurately because the playing area is so small and the ball is so light.

4 You have to train hard every day to get very strong arms if you want to be good at this sport. You also need to have very strong legs to support yourself, but you don't move around to do it.

5 People who play this sport are usually very tall, but you also have to be able to run a lot, move quickly and throw very well.

A 2 B 5 C 4 D 1 E 3

05 This exercise deals with another common task in the listening exam, listening for specific words to complete tables. Make students aware that the answers will occur in the same order as the recording and one of the sports will be used twice.

Tell students to complete Exercise 05.

Tapescript 14

OK, so when you get there you'll have to start setting up the rooms for the people taking part in the competition. I've been there and looked at the rooms and the equipment they've got is not as good as ours, but it'll be OK. There's a big store room with all the equipment in it. You should be able to get the key from reception – they'll be there waiting for us.

There are three rooms where the competitions are taking place. Remember that two of the rooms have different competitions in the morning and afternoon. So first of all, let me give you the schedule for the morning. The Dean Room is for the badminton competition. There are two courts in there, so you'll have to set up both of them. Then, the Carsley Room is where the gymnastics will be, and there's quite a lot of equipment to bring in for that. We have to get the Forster Room ready for the weightlifting, which is taking place in there all day, so once you set up the room for the weightlifting, you won't have to change anything, but there's a lot of equipment to put in there.

Now, in the afternoon, the table tennis is taking place in the Dean room, so you'll need to – oh, wait a minute, we had to change that because there are no basketball nets in the Carsley Room, so actually, the basketball will be in the Dean Room, but as the nets are already there, you won't need to set anything up for that. That means the table tennis will be taking place in the Carsley Room in the afternoon, so you'll have to make sure all the equipment is in there, as there will be a lot to do to change the room around.

| 1 badminton | 2 gymnastics | 3 weightlifting |
| 4 basketball | 5 table tennis | 6 weightlifting |

EXAM SKILLS

In this practice exam task, students are required to complete a table and a set of notes. It is particularly important with these type of exercises, that candidates read the information that is already there and then attempt to predict the type of information which is missing.

06 Tell students to predict/ guess the information, which is missing from the table/set of notes.

Tell students to listen to the recording and complete Exercise 06. As stated in *Tip 6*, students need to write the same words as heard in the recording. Candidates will be told in the instructions how many words they need to write. It is important, that students write the exact number of words requested, otherwise their answer will be marked as incorrect. Play the recording more than once, if needed.

Tapescript 15

Now about the equipment. For the badminton in the Dean Room, there are two nets in the storeroom to set up and you know what to do so it shouldn't take you long. The players will bring their own racquets with them, but there are some spare ones, so take them into the badminton room as well, just in case. There are also a couple of boxes of shuttlecocks if we need them.

For the basketball in the afternoon, you only need to bring in the balls because the nets are always up and ready, so you can do that between the sports events. In the Carsley Room, you'll have to get the gymnastics equipment in place in the morning. That means bringing in the vaulting horse and putting it in the middle. Put one mat in front and another behind the horse, and have some other mats ready for the floor exercises. Then on the side, set up the bars for the gymnastics. There are two sets of bars: one for the men and one for the women. The other equipment, such as the rings and pommel horse, are already in there, so you don't need to worry about those. It's also a good idea to bring in the tables and nets for the table tennis at the same time. There's enough room to leave them folded while the gymnastics is going on, but you'll be able to set them up more quickly later. The players should bring their own bats with them, but there's a box of bats there, so bring those in as well as we might need them.

For the weightlifting, get someone to help you bring in the barbells and the other weights so that you don't try to carry too much. The bench for the bench press should be in there already, so check that it is when you arrive, but you'll need to bring in the stand with the chalk for the lifters to put on their hands. I'll

be there at about ten o' clock as I have an appointment first thing, so you should be ready by then. We can check everything together and then get ready to welcome the contestants and the spectators. I hope everything goes well, and I'm sure we can do it! Call me if you need any extra information.

| 1 nets | 2 balls | 3 mats | 4 bars | 5 bats | 6 bench |

Alternative

If students struggle with this, you could read the tapescript to students using a slower pace and perhaps emphasising some of the key words.

07 Exercise 07 requires students to match information to people. In this task students need to listen very carefully, as some of the sports will be mentioned several times. It isn't enough for students to listen to a name and then a sport and then link them., They have to understand the full meaning of what is being said. Again, play the recording more than once, if needed.

Tapescript 16

Hi guys, it's Jeff, again. Can you let me know when you've received this message? I've just realised that I probably won't be able to be there at the start of the competition because I have an appointment that I can't cancel, so I'm going to tell you what event I want each of you to organise during the day, just so that you know. I've tried to work it out so that each of you can be in charge of the event you prefer as far as possible. So, first of all, the morning: now, Steve and Amanda, I know that you both like badminton and Amanda, you used to do gymnastics, so I know you'd be happy with either, but I have to make sure of the best arrangement on the day. Amanda, if I remember rightly, you also once did some training in the rules of badminton, so it might be best if you take that on, rather than the gymnastics. It will be useful to have you there to help with judging line calls and so on. That means either you, Steve, or you Malik, with the gymnastics. Either of you is capable of doing that, but that leaves the weightlifting. Both of you do a lot of the general training in our sports centre, but this is a bit more specialist in terms of getting the weights right for each competitor. OK, for the moment, I'll put Steve in charge of the gymnastics and Malik can take care of the weightlifting in the morning, as I think you have just that bit more experience of dealing with weights, Malik.

For the afternoon, I know Amanda and Malik would both love to do the basketball as you both play it, but Malik, you're already doing the weightlifting, so perhaps Amanda, you can do the basketball. Actually, no, I've just thought. I'm pretty certain I'll be in for the afternoon, so Malik, you won't need to do the weightlifting then. How about you do the basketball, Malik? Then I can take over the weightlifting in the afternoon, as I'm particularly keen on that, as you all know, and I'd like a chance to get involved with it. So then, Amanda, you can do the table tennis, but that leaves Steve without anything. No, that's OK, actually, if we leave it at that. Steve, you can be available to help wherever you're needed in the afternoon, and if something happens and I can't make it in the early afternoon, you can take care of the weightlifting till I arrive, though I don't think there'll be any problems. OK, if you need to check on anything, call me on my mobile. Otherwise, see you next week. I think we're going to have a great day!

A 2	B 1,6	C 3,4	D 5

Alternative

If students struggle with this task, give them a copy of the tapescript to read and determine the answers. Once they understand how this type of question works, they will be better prepared for other tasks of this type.

SPEAKING

OUTCOMES

- express your opinions about sport for Speaking Parts 1 and 2
- use connecting words to give longer and more detailed answers
- use sentence stress and intonation to express your feelings about a topic.

OUTCOMES

The outcomes of this lesson help students to express their opinions on a topic, a requirement of all Parts in the Speaking exam. This particular unit deals with Part 1 and 2., relating to the topic of leisure and recreation.

Outcome two, specifically focuses on the use of connecting words (and, so, because etc.), in order for students to provide longer and more detailed answers. At this level, students are expected to use a range of connecting words.

Outcome three focuses on the correct use of sentence stress and intonation, two areas which candidates are assessed on.

Definition

Sentence stress: the parts of the sentence you give most emphasis to.
Intonation: the way your voice goes up and down when you speak.

If used incorrectly, they can both have an impact on the meaning of a sentence.

Intonation

e.g. You don't like this, do you?

If the intonation goes up at the end, the speaker is asking the question and requesting an answer.

If the intonation goes down at the end, the speaker is making a statement and not requesting an answer.

Sentence stress

I didn't choose to watch THIS channel- implies the speaker dislikes the channel.

I didn't CHOOSE to watch this channel- implies the speaker was forced to watch this channel.

LEAD-IN

01 Tell students to match the activities in the box to the photographs. This exercise aims to engage students in the topic of leisure and recreation, subjects, which may feature in the exam.

A hiking	B movies	C karate / kickboxing	D swimming
E football	F video games	G surfing the internet
H gym	I reading

02 Students ask and answer questions 1-3 in pairs. Monitor students and assess how comfortable they are with expressing their own opinions. Make sure students are providing fairly detailed answers and not just producing yes or no.

Advice

Some students are less comfortable with expressing their opinions, even in their own language. It is important therefore, that these students are given plenty of practice to develop this skill, before the exam.

Extension

You could then ask students to report to the class on their partner's answers.

E.g. My classmate, Tom, really likes to play football in his free time, in fact he plays every Saturday for a local team.

03 Draw students' attention to *Tip 3*. In order to achieve a good mark, students must use a wide and varied vocabulary.

Tell students to read the vocabulary in Exercise 03 and match the phrase to the correct column. If needed, complete as a whole class.

👍	⁉️	👎
I like …	I don't know if I like …	I don't look forward to …
A lot of people like …	I'm not sure whether I like …	I hate …
I'm very keen on …	I don't know much about …	I'm not a big fan of …
I often enjoy …	I'm not really interested in …	Not many people like …

Advice

Make students aware that this is very useful vocabulary for the speaking exam and these phrases can be used to discuss any topic.

Extension

In order to get students using this language, you could ask them to complete these sentences (keeping to the unit topic) and then discuss their sentences with a partner.

E.g. I'm very keen on football/ I'm not really interested in motor racing.

04 Exercises 04-08 practise the use of four very important connecting words: and, but, so & because. It is important that students use these correctly in the exam, in order to produce longer and more detailed sentences. Draw students' attention to *Tip 4*. In the exam, students will be expected to use a range of simple and complex grammatical structures in their answers.

04

> **Sample answers**
>
> 1 I love listening to K-Pop BECAUSE it's really exciting.
> 2 I sometimes enjoy mountain climbing BUT I prefer water sports.
> 3 I don't like spending money SO I prefer staying at home.
> 4 I'm not really interested in watching football on TV AND my friends don't really like it either.

05 Exercise 05 gives students an opportunity to use connectors in statements about themselves.

In order to give candidates some examples, you could model a few sentences about yourself.

e.g. I like dancing and my friends like it too

Tell students to complete Exercise 05 and then select some students to read out their sentences, to check these connectors have been used correctly.

06 Tell students they are now going to produce sentences, which combine the connecting words, as this is more likely in natural speech. Again, provide students with some personalised examples on the board.

e.g. I like going out dancing and socialising with friends, but I don't stay out too late because I like my sleep, so I always get home by 10.00.

Tell students to complete exercise 06 and then ask some of them to read out their sentences.

07 As demonstrated in exercise 6, students will often have to provide reasons for their statements/opinions. Exercises 07 & 08 practise this skill. Draw students' attention to question 1 and ask candidates to brainstorm ideas for liking swimming.

e.g. good exercise, relaxing, keeps you cool in the heat.

Complete question 1 as a whole class, then ask students to complete exercises 2-4.

> **Sample answers**
>
> 1 I like it because it's cool in summer, keeps me fit and is good for my back.
> 2 I enjoy it because it's exciting, I can follow my favourite team and it's cheaper than going to the match.
> 3 I love it because it's relaxing, good for my vocabulary and inspiring.
> 4 This is because I love good stories, special effects and to escape my everyday life!

Tell students to complete Exercise 08 in the same way as exercise 07.

09 This exercise will help students generate ideas and opinions on sport and famous sporting events, themes they could be asked to discuss in the exam.

Tell students to complete Exercise 09 in pairs. Remind them to make their answers as complete as possible and to avoid Yes/No answers. They should also try to use connecting words and give reasons for their answers, where appropriate.

10 Check that students remember the meaning of Sentence Stress and Intonation, which was outlined at the beginning of the lesson.

Draw students' attention to the information box, stating that English speakers stress the content words in a sentence, and leave the function words (like, the, of etc.) unstressed.

e.g. I love going to the cinema, especially to see horror films.

Content words are words such as nouns, verbs and adjectives, words which carry meaning. In this case, love, cinema and horror are the content words.

Tell students to listen for the stressed words in *Exercise 10*.

Tapescript 17

1 I think that rowing is a great sport if you want to stay fit and healthy.
2 I often enjoy tennis as it is very competitive and I like to beat my friends.

Alternative

Ask students to listen to the sentences and then repeat using the same sentence stress.

11 Tell students to look at the first sentence in Exercise 11 and predict which words the speaker might stress. (i.e. which are the content words?)

Tell students to listen to sentence 1 and check their answers.

Play the rest of the recording and tell students to underline the stressed words in each sentence.

Tapescript 18

> 1 Ryan **Giggs** was a **famous player** for Manchester **United**; he played **hundreds** of games.
> 2 At London **2012**, the United **States** was **top** of the **medals** table, followed by **China**, then Great **Britain** and Northern **Ireland**.
> 3 Last **weekend**, I was going to go to the **gym** but I **decided** not to **bother**.
> 4 Michael **Jordan** is the **number one all-time points scorer** in the NBA **playoffs**, although Lebron **James** is catching up.
> 5 I ran in the **London marathon** last **year**. I thought I was **never** going to make it to the **end**!

12-14 Exercises 12-14 focus on helping students to recognise and produce correct intonation patterns; something examiners look for when assessing students.

Tell students to read statements 1-4 in exercise 12 and decide whether the sentences are positive or negative in tone. Elicit from students which words helped them decide on the answer.

e.g. 1. favourite/ amazing- positive.

12

> 1 positive   2 negative   3 negative   4 positive

Tapescript 19

1 My favourite sport is hockey. It's amazing!

2 I like swimming, but I wish there were more places to swim where I live.

3 I've always liked fishing but I don't have time to do it anymore.

4 I'm really excited about all the new video games that will come out soon. I can't wait!

13 2 I like swimming, but I wish there were more places to swim where I live.

3 I've always liked fishing but I don't have time to do it any more.

4 I'm really excited about all the new video games that will come out soon. I can't wait!

14 Monitor students' pair work.

15 Exercise 15 provides students with a useful selection of sports verbs. Students need to learn how to use these verbs correctly in order to comfortably talk about this topic in the exam. Elicit the meaning of any unknown vocabulary.

Extension

To ensure the correct use of these verbs you could ask students to create their own sentences and personalise the topic.

e.g. When I was younger, I used to beat my brother at pool. He wasn't very happy about it, because he likes to win.

> **Sample answers**
>
> 1 I didn't think Mayweather would [beat / defeat / lose to / knock out] Pacquaio in that boxing match.
>
> 2 It has always been a dream of mine to [play / compete / qualify / win / represent my country] at Wimbledon.
>
> 3 I try to [exercise / train / compete / play] about three times a week, so that I can keep playing well.
>
> 4 I [support / watch] Liverpool Football Club. I've been a fan for a very long time.
>
> 5 Their international football team [shoot / tackle] plenty of times during a game but usually [score] very few goals.

EXAM SKILLS

16-17 Tell students they will now complete a practice exam task in pairs. Exercise 16, gives an example of Part 1 and exercise 17 gives students an example of Part 2.

The tasks will be timed and for part 2 (ex17) they will have one minute to prepare notes, before speaking for two minutes. One student will speak, whilst the other keeps time and listens. Students will then exchange roles.

Tell students that they will be monitored on the following: their use and range of vocabulary
their ability to provide complete answers, including reasons
their use and understanding of connecting words
their use of sentence stress and intonation.
a clear structure, with the logical progression of ideas

Extension

Choose a few of the student pairs to demonstrate their answers to question 16 & 17 to the whole-class.

READING

> **OUTCOMES**
>
> - match information in a question with information in a text
> - skim a text to identify types of information
> - recognise the passive.

OUTCOMES

Draw students' attention to the outcomes of the lesson, the first two of which focus on the exam task of matching information in a question with information in the text. The second outcome teaches students how to locate the answer quickly, by skimming the text and identifying the type of information in each paragraph. Timesaving skills are very important in the reading exam, as the time limit is one of the most challenging aspects for candidates.

Tell students that this unit focuses on *The News & Media*, a subject, which may arise in any part of the exam. Elicit sources of news and media and ask students how they consume the news (e.g television, radio, newspapers, ipads, smartphones etc..)

LEAD-IN

01 Tell students to read the quotes in Exercise 01, expressing different opinions on how the news is consumed. Elicit the meaning of any unknown words.

02 Tell students to match statements 1-4 with quotes A-D. Draw students' attention to *Tip 2*, stating that this type of task may feature in the exam. The texts will be much longer however and they will need to match a question to a paragraph. The statements will paraphrase the meaning of the information in the text.

> **Definition**
>
> Paraphrase: to express something that has been said or written in a different way, usually so that it is clearer

1 A	2 D	3 C	4 B

Alternative

With a weaker class you could ask students to first underline the key words in the statements 1-4 and then ask them to match these words to parts of the text.

e.g continual exposure- 24hrs a day, 7 days a week

03 Tell students to complete *this* exercise, by discussing whether they agree/disagree with the quotes in Exercise 01. Make sure they also give reasons for their answers. Monitor students and ask some of the stronger pairs to demonstrate their discussion.

Extension

Students could also discuss whether or not these quotes reflect the opinions of the people they know, in these particular age groups.

04 In this exercise students are going to practise matching information in the question with information in a paragraph; a task, which features in the exam.

05 Tell students to skim the text to understand the general meaning of each paragraph and then complete Exercise 05. Elicit the meaning of skimming and how this can be achieved.

> **Sample answer**
>
> to read the text quickly for the general idea, by focussing mainly on key words.

Make sure that they read the instructions carefully, which state that they can write any letter more than once.

1 B	2 A	3 D	4 D

06 This exercise gives students some important information, which they must remember about this task type. Students need to consider their answers to Exercise 05 and then decide if each statement is True or False.

1 T	2 T	3 T	4 T	5 T

Advice

It is important that students remember these points, particularly statement 1, as this is one of the few tasks where the answers do not follow in the same order as the text. If students do not remember this, they may struggle in the exam.

07 This exercise focuses on the importance of synonyms in this task type. Like many of the reading exercises, the words in the question are rarely the same as those in the text. An understanding of this is key to being successful in the reading exam.

Tell students to complete the table in this exercise with the missing words/ phrases from either the text in Exercise 04 or question in Exercise 05. If appropriate, complete gap 1 as a whole class.

1 the most popular way	2 66%	3 several methods
4 25%	5 survey	6 on a weekly basis

Advice

When recording new vocabulary, tell students to form the habit of also making a note of synonyms. An awareness and knowledge of synonyms will help them greatly in the reading exam, as they are a feature in the majority of tasks.

| 1 the most popular way |
| 2 66% |
| 3 several methods |
| 4 25% |
| 5 survey |
| 6 on a weekly basis |

With a weaker class, you could write the synonyms on the board, for them to choose from.

08 Draw students' attention to the information box, stating that one way of saving time in the matching information task is to identify the type of information in each paragraph. Once the purpose of the paragraph is identified, it can then be matched to the statement with the same/similar purpose. Make sure students are familiar with all of these categories.

Exercises 08 & 09, practise this idea of labelling the type of information featured in each paragraph. Complete question 1 as a whole class. Elicit from students which words helped them choose the type?

e.g. left shocked- reaction

| 1 reaction | 2 opinion | 3 cause and effect |
| 4 summary | 5 description | 6 account |

09

| B reason / factual | C cause and effect |
| D problems / factual | E opinion | F summary |

GRAMMAR FOCUS: THE PASSIVE

Exercises 10 to 13 focus on the use of the passive. The passive is used regularly in news sources to express a sense of formality. It is important that students recognise this tense in the reading, as it says a great deal about the tone of a text. If needed, do the first question of each exercise as a whole class, in order to give students an example.

10

| 2 it was also revealed – past simple passive |
| 3 social networks are being used selectively – present continuous passive |
| 4 there has been growing concern by researchers – present perfect passive |

11

| The passive voice is commonly used in formal writing. Also in sentences 1–3, the agent is not important (e.g. in sentence 1 we are not interested in *who* uses social media to break news). |

12

| 2 has been delayed (present perfect) / is delayed (present simple) |
| 3 were named (past simple) |
| 4 is being developed |

Extension

If some students struggle with this task, you may want to discuss which words in these statements indicate the use of a certain tense.

e.g

3 earlier this morning- past simple

13

| 1 … is blamed for all the wet weather. |
| 2 … was found unconscious in his Manhattan apartment. |
| 3 … has been recovered from a sunken Spanish ship. |
| 4 … is being celebrated today. |

14 This exercise assesses how much the students have learnt about this particular exam task, throughout the lesson. Tell students to complete Exercise 14.

| 1 Questions and instructions | 2 Synonyms | 3 No |
| 4 Yes | 5 No |

Alternative

This could also be done as a short class quiz.

EXAM SKILLS

15 Set a time limit and tell students to complete this practice exam task. (suggested time limit, 7 mins)

Alternative

With a weaker class, ask students to firstly underline the key words in the questions before attempting the task.

| 1 E | 2 A | 3 B | 4 C | 5 F | 6 B |

WRITING

OUTCOMES

- use time markers and the passive to describe a process
- plan a description of a process
- interpret scientific and technical diagrams.

OUTCOMES

This lesson relates to writing task 1, in which candidates could be asked to describe a process. Draw students' attention to the outcomes, which all focus on completing this task type successfully.

Outcome 1 focuses on the use of time markers and the passive, essential tools for this task type. Time markers ensure that the answer is logically organised and the use of the passive provides the formal tone, used when describing a process. Make sure students understand the meaning of time markers.

> **Time markers:** words which help describe a sequence of events e.g firstly, secondly, thirdly etc.

The second and third outcome focus on two aspects which students may find challenging with this task; planning their answer and interpreting/understanding the diagram they are given.

LEAD-IN

01 In order to get students used to the idea of describing a process, this first exercise shows the simple process of writing a local news story. Sentences a-g give students an example of how this particular process might be described.

Tell students to order the sentences, using the pictures as a guide.

Alternative

With a weaker class you could discuss the pictures first and describe what they each depict, before attempting the task.

1 e	2 g	3 c	4 d	5 a	6 f	7 b

Exercises 02-06 focus on the use of time markers. At this level, students are required to use a range of vocabulary to produce an answer, which demonstrates a clear logical order and progression. For this type of task therefore, the use of time markers is essential.

02-03 Tell students to complete Exercises 02 & 03.

02

First, Secondly, Thirdly, Next, Then, After that

03

Set 3

04 Tell students to read the process of how a newsroom works and then the sample answer. Make sure students know how the diagram works: e.g It starts with point 1, then follows on clockwise.

Draw students' attention to *Tip 4*, stating that the wording in the diagram should not be repeated in the answer.

e.g How a newsroom works- diagram

How news stories are created- answer. Tell students to complete Exercises 05 & 06. With a weaker class answer these questions as a whole class.

05

1 No   2 No
3 Yes – although it's better to use synonyms if possible

06

Sample answers

1 First/to begin with	2 Secondly	3 Thirdly
4 Then / After That	5 Finally	

07 As with any of the writing tasks, planning is an essential part of answering the question. Draw students' attention to the information section, stating that planning will not only ensure the answer is logical and structured, it may also help them to understand the question more and choose the most significant features.

This exercise gives students a suggested plan for describing a process. Tell students to read this carefully. They will need to remember to come up with and follow a plan like this in the Writing exam.

08 In order to practise this idea of describing a process, this exercise asks students to describe some of the familiar processes from the box.

Feedback

As students are describing some of these familiar processes, monitor their use of time markers and structure.

09 Tell students to write a plan (like the one in Exercise 07) for one of these processes.

Knowledge of the passive tense is essential for this task, as when writing about a process the style must be formal.

GRAMMAR FOCUS: THE PASSIVE

10 Tell students to underline the use of the passive in the diagram in Exercise 04 and elicit which passive tense has been used.

> Present simple passive (are assigned, are booked, are allocated, is reviewed are loaded ... saved); passive used with a modal: can be cut

11 Tell students to complete Exercise 11. Do the first sentence as a whole class.

> 1 A local news story is chosen.
> 2 The story is accompanied by a picture.
> 3 A good first line is thought of.
> 4 The main body of the article is written.
> 5 The article is checked for errors.
> 6 A good title is invented.
> 7 The article is submitted to a local newspaper.

12 Draw students' attention to the information box, stating that although diagrams given in this task can vary, they are often technical or scientific. It is important that students are made aware of this, so they know what to expect in the exam. As stated in *Tip 12*, students are not expected to have any previous knowledge of the subject. The answer is purely based on their interpretation of the diagram given.

Exercise 12 gives students some strategies to deal with this. Tell students to read and order the steps.

A 3	B 5	C 2	D 4

EXAM SKILLS

13 Give students this timed writing task. Some useful verbs and phrases have been supplied here, which will help students describe this particular process. Make students aware that this will not be the case in the actual exam. Elicit the meaning of any unknown words.

Tell students that when you mark their essays you will be looking for the following:

the use of time markers to determine a clear structure to their essay

the correct use of the passive

an accurate interpretation of the process

Sample answer

The diagram illustrates a method called 'lithography', a process used for printing newspapers. After the image is transferred onto a press plate, it goes through several rollers before being successfully printed onto paper.

First, the plate is passed through dampening rollers, which provide a mixture of water and chemicals. This is to dampen the non-image areas. Secondly, the plate passes through a set of ink rollers, in order for the ink to stick to the image area. Thirdly, the plate then goes through the blanket cylinder. This is to squeeze out the water and the inked image area is picked up. Finally, the plate passes through the impression cylinder. The paper then runs between the impression cylinder and blanket cylinder, pressing the image onto the paper. After that, the paper is dried with hot and cold air and put on the delivery pile. Overall, the diagram shows that there are four sets of rollers used, before the image is transferred onto paper.

LISTENING

OUTCOMES

- identify the attitudes and opinions of speakers through expressions and intonation
- recognise paraphrases off what speakers say
- understand the role of distractors when answering multiple–choice questions.

OUTCOMES

Draw students' attention to the outcomes of this lesson, which explore three of the key skills needed for the listening exam: identifying the opinions/attitudes of speakers, recognising paraphrasing and understanding the role of distractors.

The first outcome deals with how students can identify the opinions/ attitudes of speakers by listening for certain expressions or recognising intonation patterns.

Check students understand the meaning of "intonation."

Intonation- the rise and fall of the voice when speaking.

This is particularly useful for students in Sections 1 and 3 of the listening test, when the speakers are often trying to reach an agreement or make a decision. Having an understanding of the speakers' opinions can help students tackle these questions c.

The second outcome explores paraphrasing, as this is often a feature in the exam, and students must be able to understand it. Check students understand the meaning of paraphrasing.

Paraphrasing- to express something that has been said or written in a different way, usually so that it is clearer.

The third outcome focuses on the role of distractors, within multiple-choice questions. Distractors will always feature in this type of questions, so it is vital students understand this concept and think carefully before choosing their answer.

Make sure students understand the meaning of 'distractors.'

Distractors- the incorrect option in multiple-choice questions. Designed to distract students from choosing the correct option.

LEAD-IN

01 In this exercise, students need to listen for the main idea in each discussion. This is an important skill for students to acquire, as they must learn to focus on the key points and not be distracted by other minor comments if they are to be successful in the exam.

Tell students to listen to the three short discussions and choose from either A, B or C for each. Students must listen carefully and not choose an answer based on the first thing they hear.

Tapescript 20

Discussion 1

A: All I'm saying is that if this government wins the election tomorrow, I think they'll just continue with the same things they've been doing over the last five years and make the economic situation worse in this country. People are already finding it difficult to live with prices going up and salaries staying the same.

B: I don't think they'll win. People have had enough and are ready to vote for a change. I hope they do. If the other party gets in, it'll be like them winning the World Cup!

Discussion 2

A: Yeah, I saw it last night. I think it was really good the way that all the characters were actually well developed and interacted with each other. The danger with that kind of film is that the science fiction aspect just takes over and you get spaceships and battles with aliens who are trying to take over the Earth.

B: I'm going to see it tonight. I listened to the review on the radio this afternoon and the critic really liked it, which is unusual because he doesn't usually recommend big commercial projects, which just aim to make as much money as possible.

Discussion 3

A: Did you see that report on the news tonight – the one about the robot football competition?

B: Yeah. It was quite amazing. I mean, it wasn't like real football, but it is amazing what they can get machines to do with the right programming these days. I mean, those robots can detect the ball as it moves around the pitch and pass it to each other. And that winning goal was like Messi scoring!

A: Yeah, I can see it becoming a real money-making business, just like the real thing!

1 B	2 C	3 A

02 Exercises 02-06 help students to understand the attitudes and opinions of each speaker. Elicit from students why this is important for the exam (speakers are often trying to reach a decision).

Focus students' attention on *Tip 2,* which states that attitude can be displayed through intonation, as well as the expressions a speaker uses. Check students remember the meaning of 'intonation', outlined at the beginning of the lesson.

Tell students they are going to listen to three speakers and they have to identify whether the tone is positive, negative or neutral.

Alternative

For weaker students, you may need to check they understand the meaning of each. In order to express this clearly, you could present students with the following diagram:

Negative	Neutral	Positive
☹	😐	☺

Example

Negative- I don't like this

Neutral- I don't mind this

Postive- I really like this

Tapescript 21

Topic 1: Modern art

Speaker 1: I don't really have much of an opinion about it. As far as I'm concerned, if it appeals to someone, that's fine. If it doesn't, then why should anyone complain about that? Personally, I like some of it, but I'm not really bothered. I can take it or leave it.

Speaker 2: Well, from what I can see, you have a lot of people looking at it and talking nonsense about how good it is. Then you also have people with too much money and too little sense, who are prepared to waste their money on this stuff. It's ridiculous! There's no comparison with the great art of the past few centuries.

Speaker 3: Oh, I think not enough people appreciate it. They look at it and think, well, my kid could do that. They think that something from the eighteenth or nineteenth century is true art and they don't understand that art develops and changes over time. These artists today are just as skilled and creative as those in the past and they should be appreciated for what they do.

Topic 2: Combating climate change

Speaker 1: It's so important that we tackle this issue head-on. We can't let it go on any longer without taking action. All the science shows that it's going to get out of control if we fail to act. The government should be supporting renewable forms of energy and we really need to reduce our dependence on oil and gas. I just wish other people could see that!

Speaker 2: There's so much nonsense spoken about it. Really, I can't understand why people get so upset about it. They quote all kinds of studies, but they don't amount to anything real. If you ask me, the climate is getting colder, at least in this country. Look at the amount of snow we had last winter! They just want to scare people for no reason.

Speaker 3: I'm not really convinced either way, actually. I mean, there are arguments on both sides, but I think it's still too early to tell. Yes, we can see that the weather in different parts of the world is becoming more extreme, but if you ask the climate experts, they never say that it's definitely climate change and just say they need more time to be sure. So that's where I am at the moment.

> *Topic 1: Modern art*
> **Positive:** Speaker 3
> **Negative:** Speaker 2
> **Neutral:** Speaker 1
> *Topic 2: Combating climate change*
> **Positive:** Speaker 1
> **Negative:** Speaker 2
> **Neutral:** Speaker 3

03 Focus students' attention on the picture of space.

Extension

In order to involve students in this topic before listening to the recording, you could ask the following:

Would you like to travel to space? Why/ why not?

Which planet would you travel to and why?

This could be done as a whole class activity or discussed in pairs.

Tell students to listen to the recording and choose either A,B or C.

Tapescripts 22

Maria: Hello Simon.

Simon: Hi Maria.

Maria: OK. What topic do you think we should choose for the project we're starting next week? I think we need to make sure that it's going to last over the next few months so that we can complete the project.

| | Simon: | Well, there are several possibilities. Have you heard of the Pluto expedition? The spacecraft is about to arrive there and it's going to send back pictures that we've never seen before. It should be really interesting. |

Simon: Well, there are several possibilities. Have you heard of the Pluto expedition? The spacecraft is about to arrive there and it's going to send back pictures that we've never seen before. It should be really interesting.

Maria: That sounds like a good idea. What do you think, Dr Thornton?

Dr Thornton: Well, I'm not so sure about that one. I mean, it's already been going for ten years and I think we should look at something which is planned for the future, but hasn't started yet. It would give you a better chance to study it in depth and do far more analysis for your monthly update reports.

Simon: I don't think that's a problem. There'll be a lot of coverage on the news over the next few weeks.

Maria: Hmm … that's true … but we really need something to last for a few months. On second thoughts maybe Dr Thornton's right. Perhaps we should look at something which hasn't started yet. Isn't there something I heard about a new Mars expedition? I think there's a group of people out in America somewhere who are preparing for a trip to Mars.

Simon: Yes. It was in the news last week. They've built a sort of camp in the desert in Arizona. There are ten people living there for six months, just like they would be together on the trip to Mars and after they arrive there.

Dr Thornton: That'd be ideal. Six months is just right for you. You could follow their progress and how the project develops. From what I know, the Pluto project is already a success, but with the Mars one you can assess how successful it is as it progresses and you can write it up for your final report.

Maria: Hmm … yeah … that sounds promising.

Simon: OK, but before we decide, I'd just like to mention one more. I heard that the Chinese are planning an expedition to the moon.

Maria: What? Another man or woman on the moon? That's already been done. I don't think the moon's particularly interesting these days.

Dr Thornton: Simon has a point. I mean, the Chinese are coming up now and they've got some new ideas. I don't think they're sending any astronauts. I think it's just an expedition with robots and machines to find the best place to start a colony.

Maria: Yes, but I don't think that's particularly interesting. I mean, no one has ever seen Pluto close up and no one has tried to go to Mars, so I think they'd be more interesting expeditions to do.

Simon: You have a point. Perhaps it would be better to focus on one of the other two.

Dr Thornton: OK, if you ask me, I'd prefer to see how a group of people get along living together in a difficult situation, like they'll be doing in Arizona in preparation for their trip. I think you'd get far more out of that, but the final decision is yours. What do you think?

Maria: I agree. I'd prefer to go for that one.

Simon: So that's agreed then. Good. Let's make a start.

Dr Thornton: Excellent. I'll make a note of that. We'll meet again next Wednesday and you can give me your project outline. I'm looking forward to seeing it.

B

04 Tell students to listen to the recording again and complete the table. Remind students to listen carefully, not to write down the first thing they hear and not to be distracted by extra information.

	Pluto expedition	Mars expedition	Moon expedition
Simon	Positive	Neutral	Neutral
Maria	Positive	Positive	Negative
Dr Thornton	Negative	Positive	Neutral

05 Exercises 05 & 06 focus on expressions, which may be used to show attitudes or opinions. Being able to recognise some of these expressions, may help students choose the correct answer in the exam.

Tell students to listen to the recording and choose the correct option, A,B or C.

Tapescript 23

Conversation 1

A: It looks like the government is going to raise taxes in the budget tomorrow.

B: Seriously? I really don't see how that could be a good idea. It'll reduce spending and affect the economy without a doubt.

Conversation 2

A: They just said on the local news that the bus companies are planning to reduce fares for travel after ten o'clock to get more people to come into town.

B: That certainly sounds like it would work well. It would definitely help shops and businesses, as well as the local attractions.

Conversation 3

A: Oh no, not again! The air traffic controllers are going on strike. That will cause massive delays at the airports and ruin a lot of travel plans.

B: Well, to be honest, I'm not really worried. I'm travelling by train for my holiday.

Conversation 4

A: It says here in today's paper that the government is going to offer free dental checks to people over 60.

B: I'm all for that. Anything that helps people take care of their teeth has to be a good thing.

Conversation 5

A: There's a report in the sports section that says Athletic are going to buy that Brazilian striker Reginaldo for £40 million.

B: That much? I can't seriously believe that! I really don't think he's as good as the experts say he is.

Conversation 6

A: The government is going to bring more doctors and medical staff from abroad to fill vacancies. Maybe they should try to find more here.

B: It's all the same to me. As long as they're qualified and speak good English, it shouldn't matter where they're from.

| 1 B | 2 A | 3 C | 4 A | 5 B | 6 C |

06 Tell students to listen to the conversations again and complete the table with the key words and expressions, which represent a positive, negative or neutral attitude.

Alternative

For a weaker class, you could provide students with a copy of the tapescript and ask them to underline these words/expressions and then complete the table.

Sample answers

Conversation	Key words/expressions	Positive/Negative/Neutral
1	I don't see how	Negative
2	certainly, definitely,	Positive
3	well, to be honest, I'm not really worried	Neutral
4	I'm all for that, a good thing	Positive
5	I can't seriously believe that, I really don't think	Negative
6	It's all the same to me, it shouldn't matter	Neutral

Extension

Wth a higher level class, you could brainstorm other expressions which convey a neutral, negative and positive tone.

e.g

Positive- Yes, I am sure

Negative- absolutely not

Neutral- I don't mind either way

07 Exercises 07-09 look at the role of distractors within the listening exam. Check students understand the meaning of distractors, outlined at the beginning of the lesson. Draw students' attention to the information box, which clearly defines what they are and what their purpose is.

Tell students to listen to part of the conversation again and choose the correct option, A, B or C.

Tapescript 24

Dr Thornton: That'd be ideal. Six months is just right for you. You could follow their progress and how the project develops. From what I know, the Pluto project is already a success, but with the Mars one you can assess how successful it is as it progresses and you can write it up for your final report.

Maria: Hmm … yeah … that sounds promising.

Simon: OK, but before we decide, I'd just like to mention one more. I heard that the Chinese are planning an expedition to the moon.

Maria: What? Another man or woman on the moon? That's already been done. I don't think the moon's particularly interesting these days.

Dr Thornton: Simon has a point. I mean, the Chinese are coming up now and they've got some new ideas. I don't think they're sending any astronauts. I think it's just an expedition with robots and machines to find the best place to start a colony.

Maria: Yes, but I don't think that's particularly interesting. I mean, no one has ever seen Pluto close up and no one has tried to go to Mars, so I think they'd be more interesting expeditions to do.

Simon: You have a point. Perhaps it would be better to focus on one of the other two.

Dr Thornton: OK, if you ask me, I'd prefer to see how a group of people get along living together in a difficult situation, like they'll be doing in Arizona in preparation for their trip. I think you'd get far more out of that, but the final decision is yours. What do you think?

C is correct

08 Tell students to complete Exercise 08. If needed, students can look at a copy of the tapescript to answer these questions.

1 She mentions that the Pluto project is successful, but doesn't say the same about the Mars project, so A cannot be right.

2 There is information about using robots and machines to start a colony, but that is connected with a Chinese project on the Moon, so B cannot be correct.

3 C must be correct, because the Mars project will last six months and Dr Thornton says that is just the right length of time for the group.

09 Make students aware of *Tip 9*, which reminds them that when they have chosen their answer, they should always check it is correct, by understanding why the other two options are incorrect. This exercise practises this skill.

Tell students to listen to the recording and choose the correct answer. Once you have checked the answers as a whole class, ask students to discuss why the other options are wrong. This can be done in pairs or as a whole class.

Tapescript 25

Dr Thornton:	I assume you've seen the latest update from the Mars project? One of the people has had to leave the project in Arizona, which is a bit of bad news. It only came out last night.
Maria:	Oh, really? We missed that. Who is it?
Dr Thornton:	Alfonso, the biologist. That means that they won't be able to monitor the plants they've been growing for food. Apparently, his mother was taken ill, so he decided it was more important to be with her than stay with the project.
Simon:	His mother's ill? That's a pity. I hope it's nothing serious. Are they planning to bring someone else in, or have they got someone to take over the plant care?
Dr Thornton:	Well, as you know, according to the rules of the project, no one else can come in once it's started, so they'll just have to make the best of it. After all, in a real situation, you can't just call up an agency and get someone else.
Maria:	I think Carla would be the best person to take over. As chief medical officer, she's had training in biology.
Simon:	That might be true, but I'm not sure that means she's the best person for the job.
Maria:	Why not? There's nobody else in the project who's got her experience in that area.
Dr Thornton:	Maybe, but I personally think the best solution would be to share the work. I'm sure they can all learn how to do it, and what's more, they can make sure that if anything else happens to one of them, the others will have a good idea of what to do.
Simon:	Yeah, I agree with Dr Thornton. That would be the best solution. But I'm sure they'll announce their plans later.
Dr Thornton:	Right, so now that update is out of the way, let's see what other progress you've made …

1 **Correct answer:** B
   Distraction: A
   (The participant's mother is ill, not the participant, so it is a problem unconnected to the project.)

2 **Correct answer:** B
   Distraction: A
   (Dr Thornton clearly states that no one else can come in once the project has started.)

3 **Correct answer:** B
   Distraction: A
   (Simon agrees with Dr Thornton, who says the work should be shared.)

10 Exercises 10 & 11 focus on paraphrasing. Check students remember the meaning, outlined at the beginning of the lesson.

Tell students they are going to listen to an example of paraphrasing and then choose the correct option A, B or C. Focus students' attention on *Tip 10*, which reminds students that in multiple-choice questions in the Listening there is always one correct answer and two distractors.

The information box below the question gives students the correct answer and the rationale for why.

Tapescript 26

Simon:	OK, so the latest from the project is that one of the people taking part, Joe, attacked another person on the team, Martin, and hit him. I really can't believe that Joe would do something like that! He's been the quietest up until now.
Maria:	Sometimes that's what happens. You think someone is OK, but it turns out that they're not. Why did he do it? Is it anything to do with personality problems, or is it just a disagreement about something?
Simon:	Well, there are strong signs that there've been some emotional or psychological problems which result from being isolated for so long.
Maria:	Isolation? What, so you're saying that Joe might be suffering some kind of psychological problems? I can see how that can happen in an environment like that, where there's no escape from the situation …

Tell students to listen again, to find the phrase in the recording, which determines B as the correct answer. (answer in bold in the tapescript above)

11 Tell students to listen to the next part of the conversation and choose the correct option

Alternative

Before the feedback stage, ask students to discuss their answers in pairs.

As shown in Exercise 10, they must also explain why the other options are incorrect. Students may need the tapescript for this, so they can underline the sentences/phrases relevant to the correct answer.

Tapescript 27

Dr Thornton: Well, as psychology tutor, I find that really interesting. Many types of people participate in projects studying the effects of isolation. We all know that one of the main issues with a project like this is how people will get on when they are locked away together for such a long time. It can produce all kinds of psychological and emotional problems. That's what I'm particularly interested in and one of the reasons why I wanted you to do this particular project.

Simon: Me too. That'll be one of the most important things to come out of this project – how people can control their emotions and feelings over a long time when they can't get away from each other.

Maria: True, but we have to remember that this is a science project and not some soap opera or television series with lots of silly people locked up in a big house or something.

Dr Thornton: I can see what both of you are saying, but there are always going to be problems like these so it's not surprising when they happen. In fact, this is the first time someone has got really angry in the first three months, so I think that's quite a positive thing.

Maria: So what do you think will happen? Will they make him leave?

Simon: I don't think they can. It's all part of the programme. And anyway, as the environmental engineer, Joe is an essential member of the team. If he left, then the whole environment of the building would go wrong, so I think they'll just have to work the situation out. Remember last month, when the ventilation system broke down? They almost lost all their fresh air. He only had a couple of hours to fix it and he managed to do it.

Dr Thornton: I'm sure they'll work it out. So what else have you found out …?

1 C   She mentions that she is a psychology tutor, and that many types of people take part in studies like this, but she is particularly interested in how people get on when they are locked away together.

2 A   She is not surprised that these problems happen. She sees Maria's point that it's not a television series or soap opera, but she thinks it's positive that the first sign of anger came after three months.

3 B   Simon refers to environmental problems, but not caused by Joe. He also talks about solving problems, but this refers to the problems with conflict, not the environment. He mentions that Joe managed to repair the ventilation system.

EXAM SKILLS

12 This exercise is a practise exam task. Students should use all of the skills/knowledge acquired during the lesson to complete it.

Elicit some of the information/ skills acquired throughout the lesson:

e.g identify the attitude/ opinion of the speaker, recognise paraphrasing/ synonyms/ understand the role of distractors.

Alternative

With a weaker class, read the questions as a whole class and elicit the meaning of any unknown vocabulary., before playing the recording. You can also play the recording more than once and/or pause it after each question to discuss the answer.

Tapescript 28

Dr Thornton: So now that the project has ended, we need to review it and I can help you plan your final assignments.

Maria: Yes. I never thought that of the ten who started out only six would finish in the end, and it was really hard for them to get through the whole programme. So, what have we learnt?

Simon: Well, I've got lots of data on the environmental systems and life support, and that's the key focus of my project report, especially considering the events last week, when the whole system came close to failing.

Maria: Right. When the life support system went offline for four hours, they had to really race to fix it. If that happened on a real trip, it'd be a disaster! They could all die.

Simon: I know. It's good that they weren't actually in danger in this project, but I agree, in a real situation people could have been killed. Who would've thought that it'd be on the front page and first item on the evening bulletin? It shows how much interest there's been in the project. Anyway, I'm hoping to use the data to design a new system if it's not too difficult.

Dr Thornton: That would be challenging but fascinating at the same time. I think you'll do well with that, Simon. Personally, I'd love to focus on the particularly interesting and useful data on the health of the participants. I think it'd be worthwhile writing about the physical effects of the project, you know, how they kept healthy in the long term, even though they became ill sometimes, but also about the psychological effects of living in an enclosed group like that. It'd be interesting to see if any of them will have any long-term health changes. Would either of you like to take that on?

Simon: Well, I'm not sure if I could take that on as well as producing an assessment of the life support issues. I feel that those are more significant in view of the current developments in technology to support this kind of expedition. I've already

	looked at the latest reports in the popular science magazines, though there are some fascinating articles due in the next *Journal of Space Studies. Maybe I could beat them to it!*
Maria:	That'd be a great idea, Simon – to write an article – but for me, the main thing is the efficiency of the crew and how well they managed to perform their duties. I'm focusing specifically on their abilities to work under the stresses of living in an enclosed environment. I'm going to analyse how well they managed to maintain their effectiveness over time.
Dr Thornton:	That's interesting. Maybe you could include a section on the psychological effects of long-term isolation. Remember the incident early in the project? It'd be very interesting to follow that up with the latest developments and results. I can give you some of the latest research on the subject from other studies for you to compare. I think it would significantly enhance your research and findings.
Maria:	OK. That sounds like a good idea. It shouldn't be too difficult to develop a wider theme to include the psychological studies. I'll work out a structure for next week.
Dr Thornton:	That's great, Maria. We can meet again next Wednesday and I can help you structure it. And what about you, Simon? Do you think you have enough?
Simon:	Yes, thanks, Dr Thornton. I've got plenty to think about, especially as the study of life support was the main aim of the whole project. I could include some observations about the effects on the physical and mental health of the participants, as it's relevant.
Dr Thornton:	That's fine, then. Is there anything else you want to discuss?
Simon:	One thing I'm really surprised about, is that they managed to complete the project without any extra costs. Everyone was expecting it to go over the original $10 million. I personally thought that it might even go up to something like $12 million.
Dr Thornton:	Well, actually, it says here that the final cost was $9.5 million, so they saved half a million in the end.
Simon:	They could give that to us to fund our projects! Is there anything about future developments?
Dr Thornton:	Well, I heard that they're going to share their research results with government and private organisations. There are a few other organisations planning trips to Mars that would love to study the results. I'm not sure the government is planning anything, but they'd be interested anyway.
Maria:	What about a follow-up? Are they planning another project?

Dr Thornton:	Well, depending on the results from this one, they're going to decide whether to have another one that will last a year. Obviously, they'll have to find some more participants. Would either of you be interested in taking part?
Maria:	It depends. I wouldn't say no, but I'd have to think a long time about it. I don't know if I'd want to be cut off for so long.
Dr Thornton:	I think you should bear it in mind. It would be so interesting to see how staying in a situation like that for a year affects physical and mental health. I'd love to follow your progress myself. I might even volunteer! What about you Simon?
Simon:	Oh, you wouldn't catch me inside one of those places! I'll be happy to follow what goes on and see how the whole system works over a year, but definitely from the outside, not the inside … I wouldn't mind working for the company, though. It'd be great to study it and get paid at the same time!
Dr Thornton:	Well, thank you, both of you. You've produced excellent results and I'm looking forward to seeing your final submissions.
	red during the lesson to complete the task.

1 B	2 A	3 C	4 B	5 C	6 A

SPEAKING

OUTCOMES

- speak about the news and media for Speaking Part 1
- use adjectives and intonation to express feelings about a news story
- use paraphrase and the passive to describe an event for Speaking Part 2.

OUTCOMES

Draw students' attention to the outcomes of the lesson. The first outcome focuses on Speaking Part 1, and prepares students to speak about the news and media.

The second outcome, teaches/ practises how adjectives and intonation can be used to express feelings. Make sure students understand what intonation is. This is useful, as describing feelings/opinions on a subject, is an important feature in every part of the speaking exam.

Definition

Intonation: the way your voice goes up and down when you speak

The third outcome focuses on skills, which may be useful for Part two of the Speaking; the passive and paraphrasing. In this part of the exam, candidates only have 1-2 minutes to speak on a particular topic and therefore paraphrasing is an essential skill to have. A good command of the passive tense will also help candidates to demonstrate their grammatical range.

LEAD-IN

01 Tell students to look at the pictures in exercise 1. Elicit the meaning of each.

- Newspaper
- The internet
- Radio
- Television

In pairs, tell students to discuss questions 1-4. Remind students to make their responses as detailed as possible, perhaps including reasons for their answers.

02 This exercise focuses on the advantages and disadvantages of various media sources. In sections two or three of the speaking exam it is quite probable that candidates could be asked to discuss the advantages/ disadvantages of a particular topic.

Example:

Are there any advantages to accessing news from the television rather than any other news source?

Advice

These advantages/ disadvantage questions can also be phrased in slightly different ways. Make students aware of this and the following phrases.

Advantages

Are there any benefits to……

What are the positive aspects of…

Disadvantages

Are there any drawbacks to ….

What are the negative aspects of…

As a whole class complete the advantages/ disadvantage table on television.

Then in pairs, tell students to discuss the advantages/ disadvantages of the other three sources (radio, the internet, television) and ask them to complete the tables.

Sample answers

Newspapers		The Internet	
Advantages	**Disadvantages**	**Advantages**	**Disadvantages**
1 Professionally written	1 Only one opinion on a news story	1 Mostly free	1 Hard to decide which news sources to trust
2 Different types of newspaper appeal to different readers	2 Selective in what to publish	2 All content available to view easily	2 Not always suitable for children
3 A wide range of story types within one newspaper	3 Uses a lot of natural resources to produce	3 Can copy and paste text and pictures into school/ college work	3 Facts not always checked

Radio		Television	
Advantages	**Disadvantages**	**Advantages**	**Disadvantages**
1 Accessible to people of all ages	1 No visual information	1 24-hour coverage	1 Stories generally given a short amount of time
2 Can listen in the car without distraction	2 Easy to miss information	2 High-quality pictures and sound along with story	2 Often includes commercials
3 Free	3 Lots of adver-tisements	3 Often includes interviews with experts in real-time	3 Not much opportunity for interaction

03 This section of the lesson teaches students to use intonation and a range of vocabulary to describe their feelings. These are criteria use for assessment iin the exam.

Tell students to complete this exercise by describing happy news stories to their partner, using the adjectives in the box.

Alternative

Weaker students will need support with this list of adjectives. In order to help them understand the meaning of each, ask them to match each adjective to one of the following:

describes something which is pleasant or enjoyable-delightful

general terms to mean something is very good-extraordinary/ impressive/magnificent/brilliant/marvellous/outstanding/tremendous

Describes something as beautiful or attractive-stunning

Then ask students to match the following nouns to the appropriate adjective:

movie, views, race, results, achievement, evening

04 Now students have acquired some vocabulary to describe positive feelings, they are going to focus on negative adjectives.

With a different partner, students describe sad news stories using the adjectives from the box.

Alternative

Again, weaker students will need support with this list of adjectives. You could either repeat the previous exercise, using a different set of nouns or ask students to come up with their own nouns. Either way students must understand the following:

Absurd, bizarre- something is very strange and unusual.

Upsetting, distressing- makes someone feel worried, unhappy or angry

Terrible, dreadful- something which is very bad

Harmful- to cause harm

Uncomfortable- not making you feel comfortable

Disgusting- extremely unpleasant or unacceptable

05 In this exercise, students explore how intonation can also be used to express emotion. The use of intonation is important in the speaking exam and it is one of the criteria used to assess students..

Tell students to listen to the recording and choose which speaker uses the correct intonation.

Alternative

With weaker students, write the first sentence on the board and mark the intonation pattern. Elicit that generally, for a positive statement the voice goes up and for a negative statement the voice goes down.

Extension

Drill the following with students, practising the intonation pattern marked by the arrows:

I don't like the fact people read the news on their phones (falling)

I am really excited about reading tomorrow's headlines! (rising)

There is too much focus on entertainment news these days (falling)

I love switching on the news first thing in the morning (rising)

Example:

1A When the report came in to say the mission was a success, everyone felt that we'd seen something extraordinary.

Tapescript 29

1A   When the report came in to say the mission was a success, everyone felt that we'd seen something extraordinary.

1B   When the report came in to say the mission was a success, everyone felt that we'd seen something extraordinary.

2A   The disaster was a dreadful tragedy with a massive loss of life. 2B The disaster was a dreadful tragedy with a massive loss of life.

3A   I'm feeling pretty uncomfortable about the situation. I hope we can find a solution soon.

3B   I'm feeling pretty uncomfortable about the situation. I hope we can find a solution soon.

4A   The results were stunning, and the team had done a marvellous job.

4B   The results were stunning, and the team had done a marvellous job.

5A   It was such an impressive sight and the noise that followed it was tremendous.

5B   It was such an impressive sight and the noise that followed it was tremendous.

6A   This was such a bizarre event, and it's incredible that we haven't been able to find out what caused it.

6B   This was such a bizarre event, and it's incredible that we haven't been able to find out what caused it.

The sentences are spoken with the correct intonation:
2 B   3 B   4 A   5 A   6 B

06-07 Exercises 06-08 focus on paraphrasing. Check students understand the meaning of this. In Part 2 of the speaking exam, students only have 1-2 minutes to speak on a particular topic and therefore paraphrasing is an essential skill to have.

Advice

Paraphrasing also allows candidates to be able to describe what they want, even if they can't remember or don't know the exact word, they are thinking of.

e.g Headline-the main stories or titles in a newspaper.

Tell students to complete exercises 06 and 07, by paraphrasing the stories in pairs.

08 Tell students to look at the pictures in exercise 08 which describe the events of an earthquake. In pairs, tell students to describe what is happening in each picture.

Tell students to then imagine they are retelling the story to a friend.

e.g. At ten o'clock the earthquake hit, people ran trying to escape, but buildings started to collapse everywhere…

GRAMMAR FOCUS: THE PASSIVE

09 Exercises 09-11 focus on the use of the passive. Draw students' attention to *Tip 10,* which states that this tense is used to focus on "what" is happening, rather than "who", did it. This is one of the reasons it is commonly used in news reports.

Having a good command of the passive tense, means that students will be able to display a wide variety of grammatical structures, a requirement at this level.

Tell students to complete exercises 09-11.

09

1 B 2 D 3 E 4 C 5 F 6 G 7 A

10

> 2   Large numbers of rocks and stones were removed (by volunteers) to rescue people.
>
> 3   Survivors were pulled from the collapsed buildings (by rescuers).
>
> 4   Many people were injured (by falling building).
>
> 5   Survivors were taken to hospital (by helicopters).
>
> 6   Many children were left homeless (by the earthquake).
>
> 7   The city was struck (by the earthquake) at 10.00 am.

11 With exercise 11, make sure that students can just see the pictures. Monitor students carefully for their pronunciation and grammatical accuracy.

Extension

If you feel your students need more practice in this area, they could discuss other news stories from that week/ day. In groups they could paraphrase the story and use the passive to describe news stories they find interesting.

EXAM SKILLS

In Exercises 12 & 13 students are going to complete a practice exam task. Students need to use skills and knowledge acquired throughout the lesson to complete the task. As stated in *Tip 13* therefore, they must use their knowledge of the passive and the expressions they learnt in the final part of the task.

Also, make students aware, that in the exam, they will be given one minute to make notes for Part 2 of the speaking test.

After monitoring the answers to *Exercise 12*, give students a minute to write notes and then ask one candidate from each pair to answer the question, whilst the other student keeps time (1-2 minutes). Sticking to the time limit give students an idea of how long they need to speak for in the exam.

Tell students that when you monitor you will be looking for the following:

- their ability to answer all the points mentioned on the card
- their use of vocabulary/ intonation to describe their emotions
- their ability to paraphrase information
- their accurate use of the passive

UNIT/04: TRAVEL AND TRANSPORT

READING

OUTCOMES

- understand the main ideas in paragraphs in order to match headings to sections of a text
- use the past simple, past perfect simple and past perfect continuous correctly
- recognise synonyms in texts and headings.

OUTCOMES

The main outcome of this lesson is to teach students how to handle the task type, Matching Headings. In order to match a list of headings to sections of text, students must understand the main ideas in paragraphs and be able to recognise synonyms in both the question and in the reading passage. This lesson will enable students to do this.

This lesson also gives students practice of the past simple, past perfect simple and the past perfect continuous. It is important that students can recognise and understand all of these tenses, in order to fully understand the meaning of the reading texts.

Write the following sentences on the board and ask students to label them as the past simple, present perfect simple or present perfect continuous.

I am looking at my photographs because…- present continuous

Yesterday I saw the most amazing attraction.- past simple

I haven't seen it before - present perfect simple

Because I have never been sightseeing in that area…- present perfect continuous

As will be explored during the lesson, each tense helps to convey a particular meaning.

LEAD-IN

01 The first exercise gives students some useful vocabulary, connected to the unit topic Travel & Transport.

Tell students to match the words to their definitions.

> 1 h 2 a 3 i 4 b 5 c 6 j 7 g 8 d 9 e 10 f

Ask students to choose four words from the list and use each in a sentence.

e.g. I was offended when he didn't say thank you.

Alternative

For weaker students, do some examples as a whole class before asking students to form their own sentences.

When students have completed the exercise, feedback as a whole class. Check students have understood and contextualized the word correctly, and that sentences are grammatically accurate.

Extension

With a stronger class, you could ask them to use as many of these words as possible in questions, which they could then ask their partner.

e.g.

1 When you travel, do you try and integrate with the locals?

2 Do you get annoyed by cancellations, when you fly?

Advice

Make students aware that as they learn new vocabulary, they should always try to record it in context, as shown in the previous exercise.

02 Draw students' attention to the information box, stating that a common task in the reading exam is being asked to match a list of headings with the correct paragraph/section of a text. The headings summarise the main idea of the paragraph section.

Tell students to skim read the text on "*Travel Tips*". As stated in *Tip 2*, students are only reading for the main ideas at this stage, so they must ignore any unknown words. This may be difficult for some students, but make sure no dictionaries are used, as is the case in the actual exam.

Draw students' attention to the information section below the reading, highlighting the fact that the heading must summarise the whole section, not just part of it or one line. A clear example of this is also given here. Make sure students understand this concept.

03-04 Tell students to complete Exercises 03 & 04. As stated in *Tip 3/ 4*, matching words does not ensure a correct answer. In fact, the correct answer (heading) is more likely to include synonyms from words in the text.

Example: instead of mentioning "time of day" in the text, it talks about "early morning".

This will be explored further, later on in this lesson.

03
> b

04
> b

05 For this task type, understanding the main idea of a section/ paragraph, is key to choosing the correct answer.

One way to do this, is for students to practise writing their own summaries of each paragraph/ section and then trying and match them with a heading.

Tell students to practise this technique, by completing Exercises 01-03.

1 Sample answers

A Words to underline: best attractions, avoid, queues, Early morning, good time, take photographs, meet the locals

Summary: Good to get up early

B Words to underline: good idea, useful phrases, the language, as much as possible, respond, people who make an effort

Summary: Speak the language, even you make mistakes

C Words to underline: delays, cancellations, do not allow, run, not to get frustrated, unable communicate, native, more polite, more effective, body language, better trip, plans to change, funny side, wrong

Summary: Don't get upset if plans change or you can't communicate with the locals

D Words to underline: Before, find out, people and customs, integrate more easily, not do anything to offend, more you know, gaining the most

Summary: Find out as much as possible about the people and culture before you go

E Words to underline: Do not just socialise, travellers, start conversations, locals, key, best and cheapest, talking regularly, better chance of learning the language

Summary: Talk to the local people to get the most from your trip

F Words to underline: real feel, a few hours, watching daily life, colours, smells and sounds, surround

Summary: Spend time sitting and observing everyday life

3
Paragraph B vii   Paragraph C iii   Paragraph D i
Paragraph E viii   Paragraph F v

Extension

If you feel students need more practice in this area, you could use an article from a newspaper, magazine or book and ask them to write summaries for each paragraph. If you choose a topic your students are interested in, this may help them to grasp the technique better.

06 In order to involve students in the next text, ask students if they have been on any interesting train journeys? Or, if they would like to go on any?

Explain to students that The Trans- Siberian Railway, makes a journey which has been described as one of the most interesting train journeys in the world.

Tell students to skim read the text, in order to understand the general idea.

(The rest of the questions in this lesson all relate to this text.)

GRAMMAR FOCUS: PRESENT CONTINUOUS, PRESENT PERFECT SIMPLE, PRESENT PERFECT CONTINUOUS AND PAST SIMPLE

07-09 Questions 07-09 practise students' understanding and use of the tenses in the title above. It is particularly important in the reading that students understand how these tenses are used as it has an impact on students' ability to understand the text.

07
1 a past simple, present perfect
  b past simple
  c present perfect continuous, present continuous passive
2 **past simple:** past form of verb
  present perfect: *has/have* + past participle
  present perfect continuous: *have/has* + *been* + verb + *-ing*
  present continuous passive: *is being* + present participle (*-ing* form)

08
1 b 2 a 3 c

09
1 have/'ve been travelling
2 got up
3 has been cancelled
4 have/'ve been sunbathing
5 have/'ve visited
6 went

10 Another key element to being successful at the task type, Matching Headings, is recognising synonyms. As stated in the information box, the words used in the headings are very often synonyms of words used in the text.

Tell students to match words 1-7 with the correct synonym a-g.

Elicit the meaning of any unknown vocabulary.

1 f 2 g 3 c 4 b 5 d 6 e 7 a

11 This exercise gives students some useful strategies/tips in order to deal with this task type.

Tell students to put the words in the correct order in questions 1-4.

1 Do not use the same heading twice.
2 Keep track of time.
3 Read the shortest paragraph first.
4 Ignore words you do not understand.

EXAM SKILLS

12 Tell students they are going to complete a practice exam task, based on the reading passage the, Trans-Siberian Railway. Before asking students to complete the exercise, draw their attention to *Tip 12*, stating that there are more headings than paragraphs. Also, in the actual exam, the matching-heading questions always come before the text.

Tell students to complete the boxes with the correct number i-ix.

Advice

Some students may not be familiar with Roman numerals (i, ii, iii etc.) so it might be useful to practise these before the exam.

Alternative

For a weaker class you could ask students to read through each paragraph and underline key words. In pairs, students could then come up with their own headings and then share with the class, explaining the reasons for their choice. After discussing the text in detail, students could then complete the exam task.

Extension

Students could

- write the headings themselves
- find the cues in the text – we have said that they need to be aware of synonyms, but we need to look at the skill as a whole when they aren't aware of the topic.
- write their own distractors – so come up with distractors when they have found the right answer.

Alternative

- Give students the right answer and then get them to find why it is the right answer
- Give students the wrong answer (using the distractors and they have to say why it is wrong – this could be done as a whole class with the exam task blown up with the wrong answers on it or as groups)

WRITING

OUTCOMES

- study and compare two maps
- read your writing to check for spelling and grammatical errors
- improve the cohesion of your writing by organising your ideas in a logical way
- make your writing easier to understand by using cohesive devices.

OUTCOMES

This unit focuses on Writing Part 1, where students may be asked to describe one or more maps. All of the outcomes in this unit relate, therefore, to producing a successful answer for this task type.

The second outcome focuses on encouraging students to check their work once it is completed. Under exam conditions, it is easy for to make silly mistakes, which can be easily rectified, once identified.

The third outcome, deals with cohesion and teaches/practises with students how to organise their ideas in a clear and logical way. This is a key element in a successful answer.

> **Definition**
>
> Coherence: the logical progression of ideas.
>
> The fourth outcome, focuses on cohesive devices

> **Definition**
>
> Cohesive devices: words which help you link ideas together.
> e.g. however, therefore, for example, in conclusion.

Elicit other examples from students. Again, cohesion is a very important part of an exam answer. Make students aware that they will be assessed on both coherence and cohesion in the exam.

LEAD-IN

01 In Writing Part 1, students may be asked to describe one or more maps. This exercise gives students some useful vocabulary for this type of task.

Tell students to label the maps using the words from the box. Make them aware, that as stated in Tip 1, in the actual exam, some of this vocabulary may already be labelled.

> 1 stadium 2 windmill 3 skyscraper 4 residential area 5 motorway 6 east 7 north 8 fields 9 hills 10 bridge 11 river 12 farm 13 pond 14 church 15 west 16 south

For this task type, it is important that students are able to read and understand simple maps, as illustrated in the previous exercise. The maps featured in the exam can vary. For example, students could be presented with a map of a park, building, street, farm etc. Students must also carefully read any information given with the maps. For example, in Exercise 01, map 1 represents "now" and map 2 represents "twenty years ago." This timescale can vary in the exam, for example, students could be presented with a map which represents "now" and one which depicts "the future".

Advice

An important aspect of this task is that students are able to choose the most significant features to write about, as is the focus for all Part 1 Writing tasks. This is even more important, when students are given more than one map to write about, as they are aiming to write just 150 words in 20 minutes.

02 This exercise aims to practise the skill of choosing the most significant features.

As a whole class, tell students to read question 1 and the example given. Elicit which tense has been used and why.

More houses have been built (present perfect- because you are describing a present result connected to the past)

Elicit from students the form of the present perfect: subject + have/has been + past participle.

Elicit more answers for question 1, monitoring the correct use of the present perfect.

e.g. A lot more facilities have been built.

Draw students' attention to Tip 2 which states that the accurate use of prepositions of place are also important in this task.

> **Definition**
>
> Preposition of place: a word or group of words that is used before a noun or pronoun to show place.
>
> For example 'on' in 'Your keys are on the table.' is a preposition of place.

Elicit other examples of prepositions of place.

Possible answers: at, in, in between, through

Tell students to complete Exercise 02 in pairs.

Sample answers

1 A motorway has been built through the centre of the island.

A hospital has been built in the east of the island.

A skyscraper has been built in the south of the island.

2 The residential area has increased in size.

3 The farm and fields have remained the same.

The church and pond near the residential area have remained the same.

03 This exercise aims to personalize the task for students, which may make producing the target language easier and/ or more enjoyable for them..

Tell students to complete Exercise 03 by discussing the changes in their own town, over the last ten years. Some words have been provided for students to help them describe change, elicit the meaning of any unknown vocabulary. If students learn to use a varied selection of verbs accurately, they are more likely to achieve a higher score.

Feedback

Monitor students for correct use of the present perfect.

As a whole class, ask some of the stronger students to demonstrate their discussions and usage of verbs.

Extension

If you feel students need more practice at interpreting maps and choosing the most significant features, you could give them further examples to discuss. Maps of local parks, buildings, towns etc. can be easily accessed on the internet.

04 Grammatical accuracy is very important in the writing test and one of the criteria students are marked on. At this level, students are expected to produce many sentences, which are error-free. Exercises 04 to 06 focus on this aspect of the task.

Tell students to complete Exercises 04-06.

05

2 dramatically – dramatically
3 threw – through   4 significantally – significantly
5 facilites – facilities

1 changed – has changed
2 building - built
3 has built – has been built
4 has being developed – has been developed
5 was occurred – has occurred

06

1 present perfect

2 because there is a connection between the past and present

07 Another criterion students are marked on is coherence and cohesion. Tell students to read the information box, which clearly explains both terms. Exercises 08 and 09 give students an example of a sample answer, highlighting how students could organise their ideas.

Tell students to look at the two maps of Mumbai. Elicit where Mumbai is.

Tell students to complete Exercises 08 & 09.

09

1 1, (9)

2 (9) 6, 2, 4, 8, 5

3 3, 10

4, 7 (sentence 9 could go in the introduction or first paragraph)

10 Having looked at the structure, students are now going to complete Exercises 10-12, focusing on how their ideas can be joined together. Tell students to read the information box, which explains what cohesive devices are, and how they can be used to link sentences together.

Advice

It is important that students do not overuse cohesive devices and only include as appropriate.

Tell students to complete Exercises 10-12.

11

1 moreover, in addition, what is more

2 similarly

3 in particular

4 in contrast, in comparison

5 to summarise, in conclusion, to conclude

12

1 in comparison / in contrast   2 what is more / in addition / moreover   3 To summarise / In conclusion / To conclude
4 in particular   5 in contrast

Extension

In order to ensure students have fully understood the use of these cohesive devices, you could ask them to complete this extension activity.

Ask them to write about the changes in their own town (as discussed in Exercise 03), but this time, they must include some or all of the words in Exercise 12. Give students the following example:

Over the last ten years there has been a lot of development in my town. Particularly in residential areas, where more flats have been built to accommodate a growing population.

EXAM SKILLS

13 Tell students to complete the timed writing task in Exercise 13. Remind them that they should spend a few minutes reviewing their answer when they have finished writing.

Tell students they will be marked on the following:

identifying the most important features in a map

grammatical accuracy

a well organised answer

the correct use of cohesive devices to successfully connect ideas together.

Extension

In order to emphasis good practice even further, you could give students a copy of the sample answer and ask them to underline the following:

the tenses used (and discuss why they are used)

the use of cohesive devices

LISTENING

OUTCOMES

- identify the main subject of conversations
- identify the functions that speakers use
- match questions and options (e.g. solutions to advantages/ disadvantages).

OUTCOMES

Draw students' attention to the outcomes of this unit. This unit deals with, "matching questions", a task in which students have to match information on paper to information in the recording. In order to complete this task type successfully, students need to be able to identify the main subject in a conversation and identify the functions that speakers use. Both of these key skills are practised in this unit.

Definition

Functions: the purpose of a conversation e.g requesting, agreeing, complaining etc.

LEAD-IN

In order to draw students into the topic and introduce the first exercise, tell them to discuss the following questions:

What is your preferred method of transport and why?

Which method of transport do you least like and why?

What problems can you encounter when travelling?

Make students aware that these types of question could also feature in Part 2 of the Speaking exam.

In Exercise 01 students are asked to identify the main topic in each conversation.

01 Tell students to listen to the recording and match each conversation to the correct letter, A-E.

Tapescript 30

Conversation 1

A: The next bus should be here soon.

B: No, it won't. I just checked. It's due in twenty minutes.

A: Twenty? I don't believe it! It should be every ten minutes. This service is getting worse and worse!

B: You're right. It was never this bad. The bus company just doesn't care about passengers any more, as long as they get the money.

Conversation 2

A: Excuse me, could you tell me why the 4.50 train to London hasn't arrived yet?

B: I'm afraid there's been an accident on the line at the station before this one.

A: Oh, sorry to hear that. Do you have any idea when it might arrive?

B: Well, at the moment the line's closed but I've just heard that the company is arranging buses to take passengers to London. There should be one here soon.

A: Thanks for letting me know.

Conversation 3

A: What do you think? Should we take the car? It's the quickest way to get to Bristol. It's straight down the motorway. We should be there in two hours.

B: Haven't you heard? There's fog on the motorway and there are massive jams all the way down. There's really no point in driving.

A: Oh, really? Well, shall we take the train? I know it's expensive, but maybe we can get a cheaper fare. I'll have a look at the train website.

B: Good idea. At least we can get there fairly quickly and safely.

Conversation 4

A: OK, darling, I'm off to work.

B: You're not using the car, are you? Remember what the doctor said. You need to get more exercise and lose weight, especially now that your leg is better.

A: I know, but my leg hurts a bit today. I'd prefer to use the car.

B: Yes, but it won't get better if you sit in the car all day. I really think you should do some more exercise. And it's a lovely day for cycling. You can use the car when it rains.

A: OK, OK, I'll cycle today, but I'll need to use the car tomorrow as I've got a lot of things to take to work.

Conversation 5

A: I'm thinking of buying a motorbike now that I've retired. I'll have a lot of time to ride around like I used to.

B: A bike? Are you sure? I really don't think that's a good idea. They're really dangerous.

A: Only if you don't know what you're doing! I used to ride one when I was younger.

B: How long ago was that? It must be at least 30 years ago. Have you been on one since?

A: No, but I'm sure I can remember how to ride one.

B: Well, if you ask me, I think you're making a big mistake. I wouldn't get back on a bike after so much time, but it's your decision.

Conversation 1: D   Conversation 2: E   Conversation 3: B
Conversation 4: C   Conversation 5: A

Exercises 02 & 03 ask students to identify the type of function that each speaker uses.

02 Make sure students understand the meaning of all of the words in list F-J, by asking them some concept checking questions

Example:

When was the last time you persuaded someone to do something?

Tell students to complete Exercise 02.

Conversation 1: H   Conversation 2: J
Conversation 3: I   Conversation 4: G
Conversation 5: F

---

03 Tell students to read sentences 1-5 and match to a function in Exercise 02. If students aren't sure of any of the answers, tell them to leave those until last.

---

1 I   2 G   3 J   4 F   5 H

Tell students that in the exam, they may be asked to match the information they have on paper to information in the recording.

04 Tell students to listen to the conversation in this exercise and choose an option from the list A-D. Remind students, that because this is a multiple-choice question, some of the choices will be distractors and therefore they must listen very carefully. If needed, play the recording more than once. Students must also state the reason for their choice.

Tapescript 31

Sophie: So the main focus of the project is the transport system in the town. We need to look at the problem carefully and then discuss possible solutions. We have to decide which one we could recommend to a transport committee.

Robert: OK, Sophie. I think the problem is not a simple one as there are various causes that we have to discuss. I think the first one is to do with the bus service in the town. In my view, the lack of buses has meant that too many people are using their cars. The service isn't reliable enough.

Sophie: Yes, you have a point there. It would be good if we could have more buses on the road all the time, but I don't think that's the main reason for the heavy traffic and the problem won't go away just by improving bus services.

Robert: You could be right. More buses would be useful, but that's not enough to put things right. We have to remember that many people come into town by rail and the rail company has been talking about reducing staff and services because of financial problems. If that happens, then more people will use their cars to come in. We need to take that into consideration when deciding on a solution.

Sophie: Of course. I think the town council can find some extra money to support the train service because, if anything, we want to increase the service to reduce the traffic on the roads. The more people travel by rail, the less they'll use the road. And we would have the added benefit of safer roads, especially at school travel times.

Robert: True, but one good thing is that the road accident rate has been falling recently, partly due to the high volume of traffic on the roads. After all, when there's too much traffic, it moves more slowly and fewer people, especially children, are in danger.

Sophie: I realise that, but that's exactly what we have to deal with: the problem of too many vehicles coming in. I know children are safer, but the air quality is much worse. We don't want to have more medical problems like asthma and bronchitis, especially for children and older people.

Robert: True, and when I think about it, I can see that the heavy traffic means that businesses lose money, people are late for work and drivers get more stressed. So, let's think about how we can deal with that and look at the possible solutions.

C (All the other issues are mentioned, but are not the main problem under discussion, and the number of accidents has actually fallen.)

---

05 Exercises 05-08 practise matching information questions. It is important that students are familiar with their format before taking the exam.

Students will be given a list of options (A,B,C etc.) which they must match to the correct question, depending on what they hear in the recording. As stated in Tip 4, the question statements follow the same order as the recording.

Tell students to read Exercise 05, which demonstrates how this type of question will be laid out in the exam. Make sure they read the question carefully, noting that there are more locations (1-4) than needed.

Tell students to listen to the recording and complete the exercise. If needed, play the audio more than once.

Tapescript 32

Sophie: So where are the worst affected places in town?

Robert: I would say one of the worst is by the Arts Centre.

Sophie: I'm not sure about that. Statistics show that the worst place is by the town hall.

Robert: Well, as most of the traffic comes in from the east of town, that would be the Arts Centre. The town hall is further over.

Sophie: Actually, Robert, that's not quite right. The traffic gets quite bad along East Road, further out of town. It's been getting worse over the last year or so, especially by the Starview Cinema.

Robert: The Starview?

Sophie: Yes, haven't you ever been there?

Robert: No, I haven't. I thought it was by the main roundabout.

Sophie: Well, in actual fact, it's by the junction of East Road and Station Road. That's where the traffic has been getting really bad, especially in the mornings. It's especially bad for the buses coming from the station as they can't turn right into East Road to get to the centre.

Robert: OK. So that's the first bad spot, then.

Sophie: Yes. Sometimes the traffic backs up for almost a kilometre, and in the evening, when everyone is trying to get home, it gets bad all the way back to the main roundabout. It's bad in the morning and the afternoon as the traffic also comes in from the north and the south. Remember, there's Liverton to the north and Scotsfield to the south and a lot of people commute to both places for work.

Robert: That's true. I live a few kilometres down the Scotsfield Road and I have a lot of trouble coming in during the morning rush hour. It's especially bad just by the Arts Centre where the road comes into the roundabout. The buses have a lot of trouble getting through that as well. OK … so those are the two main hotspots, the Starview and the Arts Centre. I've marked them on the map. And that leaves the town hall.

Sophie: Hmm … yes. I mean, the whole area around Central Park is bad, but you're right, the town hall side of Central Park is the worst in the area. It's bad enough right by the shopping centre on the other side of Central Park, but

it's particularly bad on the town hall side, with all the heavy lorries coming into the centre from the industrial estate on the west side of town. They usually make their deliveries in the morning rush hour.

Robert: So, you're saying that if we stopped them from coming in early to the area by Central Park where the town hall is, that would make the traffic a lot lighter?

Sophie: I'm sure it would. Now that we've established where the worst places are, let's have a look at the proposals.

Location 1: B   Location 2: C   Location 4: A

Alternative

If students struggle with this exercise, provide a copy of the tapescript and ask them to underline the answers.

Advice

As demonstrated by Exercise 05, there can be a great deal of extra information in these audios, which students must learn to ignore so they can focus on what the task is actually asking for, which in this case, is location.

06-08 Exercises 06-08 give students further practice of this type of question n. Remind students to listen for only the relevant information. For example, in Exercise 06 students are only listening for solutions. Play the recordings more than once if necessary.

Tapescript 33

Sophie: The first proposal is to introduce bus and cycle lanes on the roads coming into each of the trouble spots, but I'm not really sure that that will solve the problem by itself.

Robert: What do you mean? I think it's a really good idea. I think it would help a lot.

Sophie: On the face of it, yes, but in actual fact it can make things worse. There've been a few studies of towns and cities where they've put schemes like that into operation and one serious problem is that car traffic tends to go off into the areas around town where people live, and that causes more traffic in places where there haven't been problems before. Drivers think they can find emptier roads in residential areas and it just sends the problem there instead.

Robert: Hmm … I hadn't thought about that. What about the second one, a park-and-ride scheme?

Sophie: Well, we build car parks on the edge of town where the main roads come in. When cars come into town from further out, they can park there cheaply and take special buses into the town centre. It's been quite popular in a few other towns around the country.

Robert: In some places, yes, but not in all. I've had a look at some of those schemes. The main problem is lack of take-up. Drivers just don't use them. A lot of these car parks stay empty for a long time and the buses are often less than half-full. It's not always a good use of public money, especially when drivers avoid using the services and prefer to come into town and pay higher parking fees.

Sophie: You've got a point there. We need to bear that in mind. Do you think either of the other proposals would work? I think the pedestrian area is a very interesting proposal. We could turn the whole of the centre, including the shopping areas, into a pedestrian zone and put in a one-way system round it.

Robert: I'm not convinced that would work. You'd move all the traffic further out of the centre and cause more problems. But the biggest problem would actually be with the shops themselves. It's fine to stop traffic around the shopping areas, but there would be huge problems with deliveries. Some shops could go out of business if they have difficulty getting lorries in with their goods.

Sophie: Right. I'll note that as well. The last one is a new tram system. We'll have to lay down a new line through the centre of town and also from north to south. It's quite a popular solution to traffic problems.

Robert: That may be so, but the main problem with that kind of project is the expense. The initial financial requirements would be huge and so would the maintenance expenses. It might well be far more than the council is prepared to spend on a solution.

Sophie: I'll note that as well. Which brings us to the next point, the question of cost …

1 B	2 D	3 A	4 C

Tapescript 34

Sophie: I've got the details on the cost of each of these projects. The tram system comes out as the costliest. It would cost over £20 million just to prepare the route and to lay the lines down, including widening the roads. Then there's the cost of buying the trams themselves and organising the system.

Robert: And what does it all come to?

Sophie: No less than £30 million in the end. At least that's what they need to try to keep the costs down to.

Robert: £30 million? That does seem a lot. I thought it was closer to £25 million, but clearly it isn't. And what about the cheapest?

Sophie: Well, it seems that it'd be either the bus and cycle lanes plan or the park-and-ride scheme. At the moment, it looks like the bus and cycle lanes might be the least expensive overall. The changes wouldn't be so large. They estimate

around £8 million to set up the signs, paint the roads, and so on, and at least another £2 million or so to make other changes.

Robert: So you're saying it's around £10 million? That seems quite reasonable. What about the park-and-ride scheme?

Sophie: Well, there are sites which have been identified for development to build the car parks, and as they're not in the centre, it won't cost too much to buy them, probably around £5 million. Then they'd just need to lay out the car parks and put in bus shelters, which should be around £6 or £7 million and then and get the buses. If they rent them, they could keep the costs down to around £3 million.

Robert: So, if I'm right, that comes to around £15 million for the park-and-ride in total. And then there's the pedestrian and one-way system. How does that work out?

Sophie: That's the second highest. We'd have to re-route all the traffic while the works are done, then change the roads along the routes to make it safer for cyclists, which is around £12 million. Then there are the new signs and so on, which comes to about £5 million and also the road painting and maintenance, at around £8 million.

Robert: So that's around £23 million. We might be able to manage that.

Sophie: Actually, that's £25 million, Robert.

Robert: So it is! My mistake. Maths was never my strong point!

1 F	2 A	3 B	4 E

Tapescript 35

Sophie: So we've discussed the negative aspects and costs of these proposals, but now I'd like to look at the real benefits which we think each proposal will bring.

Robert: Well, I really think that one of the most important benefits is better public transport. The most important thing is to get more people out of their cars and onto public transport.

Sophie: Well, three of the proposals would help with that – park-and-ride, bus- and cycle-only routes and the new tram transport system. Which do you think would be the best out of those three?

Robert: I think the bus and cycle routes would be great for town centre transport, but they might push car traffic further out and make it more difficult for buses outside the centre. That leads me to think that the tram system would actually improve public transport the most, even though it's the most expensive, as there will be a new form of transport in the centre, without affecting other parts of town.

Sophie:	I think you have a good point there. I agree that in the long term it would be the best thing. Do you think that proposal would also increase the number of visitors in town?
Robert:	Well, of course. Any of the solutions would do that, but I'm not sure if the tram system would be the best. What do you think?
Sophie:	I think the park-and-ride would be better than the tram system for that. The trams would help people who are already in town, but a park-and-ride would bring more of them in from outside.
Robert:	So you think the park-and-ride would bring most visitors in?
Sophie:	Actually, I think if people know that they can get around the centre more easily, do their shopping and so on, they would come in more. So perhaps the pedestrian area and one-way system would be best in that respect.
Robert:	True. I've seen other town centres become really busy when they've put in pedestrian areas, so that's clearly the best way of bringing visitors in. So we agree on that, then.
Sophie:	And I think that people's health will improve as well as they will be walking around the pedestrian area, rather than driving around town.
Robert:	Up to a point, yes, but I'm sure you'd agree that encouraging people to do more cycling would help their health far more.
Sophie:	Of course. Creating bus- and cycle-only routes would be the best way of getting people to exercise. It would also help reduce pollution, so even the people who don't cycle will breathe cleaner air.
Robert:	And we agree that producing less pollution is a really important part of this scheme, though I think that the park-and-ride would be better at doing that than the bus-and cycle-only routes.
Sophie:	I'm not sure. Lots of people would need to use the park-and-ride to help reduce pollution. Bus- and cycle-only routes keep cars out of the centre.
Robert:	Yes, but if people are encouraged to use park-and-ride more, it would produce the best results. There would be far fewer cars in the centre and the air would be much cleaner.
Sophie:	Yes, that's true, but that's a lot of work for the council. OK, we'll agree on a park-and-ride, then. What about safety? I'd say the bus and cycle routes would be best from that point of view.
Robert:	Probably. I think I agree with you on that.
Sophie:	OK then, so we agree on safety.
Robert:	Actually, no. When I think about it, you have to take pedestrians into account as well. It's safer for cyclists when there are no cars around, but I'm not sure that it's safer for pedestrians.

Sophie:	They still have to avoid cyclists, who don't always pay attention to pedestrians, so I really think the pedestrian area and one-way system would be safer for them. Cyclists won't be allowed in the pedestrian areas, so there will only be people walking.
Sophie:	Yes, you have a point there. Shall we change that then?
Robert:	OK. I'm glad you agree. So, that's all done then. We have all our recommendations!

| 1 D | 2 C | 3 B | 4 A | 5 C |

09 Elicit the meaning of each of the functions in Exercise 09. You could perhaps ask students for an example sentence for each.

e.g. proposing/suggesting- would you like to go to dinner tonight?

approving/accepting- yes, I would love to

Extension

In order to make this activity more interactive, you could ask students to write short dialogues in pairs/ groups featuring all of these functions. Students could then practise these dialogues.

Advice

Identifying the function of a piece of audio is an important skill for students to acquire and will help them follow any conversation.

Tell students to listen to the extracts and match to one of the functions (A-G.)

Tapescript 36

1 Actually, Robert, that's not quite right.

2 I think you have a good point there.

3 On the face of it, yes, but in actual fact it can make things worse.

4 What about the second one, a park-and-ride scheme?

5 Up to a point, yes, but I'm sure you'd agree that encouraging people to do more cycling would help health far more.

6 I'm not sure about that. Statistics show that the worst place is by the town hall.

| Extract 1: E | Extract 2: B | Extract 3: G |
| Extract 4: A | Extract 5: F | Extract 6: C |

Elicit from students which words/ or phrases helped them identify the correct function.

EXAM SKILLS

10 Tell students to complete the practice exam task in Exercise 10. In questions 1-3, they have to listen for the main idea in each recording and in the second exercise they have to match the statement to the option in the box.

Alternative

For a weaker class, give students a copy of the tapescript, if needed, and play the recording more than once.

Tapescript 37

Jane: Have you got the results from the survey we did about the changes that've been made to Ashtown in the last 25 years?

Bill: Yes, and there've been a lot of changes. Some of the people are happy about and some of them they aren't.

Jane: What, for example?

Bill: Well, for example the bus system used to be much better and, even though the old uncomfortable buses have been replaced with new stylish ones, fewer people use them.

Jane: Why is that?

Bill: A lot of people think it is because fares are higher, but that isn't true. In fact, the cost compared to average salaries is pretty much the same as 25 years ago. The fact is that the buses now just go to the most popular destinations and, as the city centre no longer allows vehicles, there are even fewer places where buses can go.

Jane: Most people must be happy with fewer cars in the town centre though?

Bill: I'm not so sure. Five years ago a bypass was supposed to be built so that people could easily get from one side of the town to the other, without going into the centre, but those plans still haven't happened. The biggest success in my opinion is the building of areas for cyclists. Far more people are travelling by bike and using the facilities than anybody could have imagined.

Jane: That's all very interesting, but how have the jobs that people do in the city changed? That's sure to have had an impact on what the town looks like.

Bill: You're not wrong there. The town used to be a lot more polluted due to all of the products that were made in factories here. Manufacturing is still important of course and services such as accountancy firms and website developers employ a lot of people in the town, but you only have to see the number of universities and colleges that have opened in the town in the last 25 years to see that is where most of the jobs are now.

Jane: OK, now shall we have a look at how some of the buildings have changed?

Bill: I think that first of all we should look at how the railway station has changed. As there are now fewer buses, more people drive to the railway station to take a train. Twenty-five years ago the car park was much smaller and, although it might not look very modern, most of the spaces have only been there for five years.

Jane: Oh yes, didn't the cinema used to be quite near the railway station? I suppose they built more spaces when they knocked it down.

Bill: That's right, the Grand Cinema used to be next to the railway station, but they rebuilt one exactly the same as the old one over in King Street.

Jane: What about the indoor market? My mum says there used to be an outdoor one, but that closed down a long time ago.

Bill: Yes, and when the outdoor market closed down, the indoor market became a lot more popular. Ten years ago it looked like it would close down too, as the building was really old and it had become dangerous. It used to be owned by the council, but a private business bought it and made the changes so that it could stay open.

Jane: It's good to see it's so popular still despite all of the new supermarkets in town. I bet the library isn't as popular as it used to be though?

Bill: You'd be surprised. A lot of people still use the library! Most people think that people are less keen on borrowing books than in the past, but the library has adapted to changes. It's true that fewer people go in there to borrow books, but since they made tablets and computers available, more people have started visiting it. It has really fast Wi-Fi too, so people like it because of that.

Jane: Quite a few of the factories have closed down or been sold in the last 25 years though, so what happened to all of the buildings that used to house them? I suppose they're all shut down now?

Bill: Some of them have been demolished, and some have been converted for other uses, but that isn't surprising. The thing that I found surprising was that, although education has become more important to the economy of the town, there isn't an art college any more. In fact the art college is now used as a doctor's surgery.

Jane: Oh really? Anyway, I think we need to look at how we're going to present these findings to …

| 1 C | 2 B | 3 C | 4 G | 5 A | 6 F | 7 C | 8 B |

SPEAKING

OUTCOMES

- plan your long-turn answer for Speaking Part 2
- use the correct sequencing words to give your answer a clear structure
- understand sentence stress when using sequencing words
- deal with follow-up questions after your long turn.

OUTCOMES

Focus students' attention on the outcomes of the unit, which discusses Speaking Part 2. In this part of the test students are given a task by the examiner and they have one minute to prepare their answer and then approximately two minutes to produce the answer. When students have finished, they may have to answer follow up questions from the examiner.

The aims of this lesson, therefore, focus on helping students prepare their answer, produce the answer and deal with any follow up questions.

Sequencing words are also a focus of this lesson, as they are particularly important in this long turn task type. This is because students are essentially recounting a short story and the examiner must be able to understand the structure and flow of what is being said.

> **Definition**
> Sequencing words: words which link ideas together
> e.g and, but, because, therefore

LEAD-IN

01 In order to draw students into the unit topic, ask them to look at the pictures and answer questions 1-4 in pairs.

02 Ask students what they have to do in Part 2 of the Speaking test (outlined at the beginning of the lesson)

Tell students they are going to listen to the examiner give instructions at the start of Speaking Part 2. Students need to listen to the recording and check their answers.

Tell students to listen to the recording again and complete Exercise 02.

Alternative

You could ask students to complete Exercise 02 first and then play the recording.

Tapescript 38

Now I am going to give you a topic and I'd like you to talk about it for between one and two minutes. You have one minute to think about your answer and you can make notes if you wish.

All right? Remember you have one to two minutes for this, so don't worry if I stop you. I'll tell you when the time is up. Can you start speaking now, please?

1 The examiner will give you a topic.
2 You have one minute to make notes.
3 You should make notes on the note paper provided.
4 The maximum time to talk is two minutes.
5 You should keep talking until the examiner stops you.

03 This exercise , gives students an example of the kind of task they may be given in this part of the test. Draw students' attention to Tip 3, stating that they should speak about their topic, using the order given.

04 This exercise helps students to write a set of notes about their topic. As shown in the table provided, each point should be addressed individually and in the order given on the card. As stated in Tip 4, adding questions can sometimes help students think of more to say.

Tell students to complete Exercise 04.

Extension

In order to practise the note taking section of the test further, you could give students another topic to practise.

e.g Describe the best or worst holiday you have ever had.

You should say:

- where you went/ who you went with
- why it was good or bad
- if you would do it again -why/why not

05 As stated in the information box, for this particular task type, sequencing words are very important.

Ask students for examples of sequencing words, outlined at the beginning of the lesson.

Tell students to close their books and listen to a student attempting the task in Exercise 03.

Tapescript 39

Student: I remember a trip I took last year, on the 12th August, I believe. I boarded a plane to Paris, which was rather exciting as I'd never done that before. Since I come from China it took a long time to arrive, but when I got there, the first thing I did was go to the Louvre Museum. You know, where the big triangle is by the entrance, and took some pictures. After that, I boarded a subway train to the Eiffel Tower to take more pictures. Because I was pretty hungry around that time, I went to a restaurant, although I had trouble ordering food because I don't speak any French. Once I'd eaten, I then took a tour bus to the Champs Elysées in order to do a bit of shopping, where I went on to buy as much as I could. I even bought a souvenir snowglobe for my friend Julie, as she collects them. However, when I got back on the tour bus and started taking pictures, I dropped my camera over the side, watching it break on the ground. After everything was over, I took the flight back to China. It was a great experience, although next time I think I should study some French before I go!

Ask students to look at the pictures and listen again. As they listen to the recording they have to order the illustrations.

Extension

You could ask students to discuss what was good and what could be improved, about this sample answer. Students could make notes as they listen or weaker students could be given a copy of the tapescript to discuss.

| 1 D | 2 A | 3 B | 4 I | 5 L | 6 C |
| 7 F | 8 E | 9 G | 10 J | 11 K | 12 H |

06 In this exercise students have to produce their own answer to the speaking task, using the linkers in the box. Check that weaker students understand the meaning and use of all these words. Perhaps choose the less familiar ones and ask students to write a sentence for each.

Less familiar: until, in order to, once, since, although, whether, while, yet.

07 This exercise focuses on sentence stress. Sentence stress is important, because it helps to convey the meaning of what is being said. Write this example sentence on the board and elicit from students why the two words in bold are stressed:

e.g. The **best** holiday I have had, was when I went to **Australia**.

Tell students to complete Exercise 07.

Tapescript 40

1 I boarded a plane to Paris, which was rather exciting as I'd never done that before.

2 Since I come from China, it took a long time to arrive, but when I got there, the first thing I did was go to the Louvre Museum.

3 I had trouble ordering food because I don't speak any French.

4 Once I'd eaten, I then took a tour bus to the Champs Elysées in order to do a bit of shopping.

5 As I got back on the tour bus and started taking pictures, I dropped my camera over the side.

---

1 I boarded a plane to **Paris** [stressed], which was rather **exciting** [stressed] as I had never done that before.

2 Since I come from China, **it** [unstressed] took a long time to arrive, but **when** [unstressed] I got there, the first thing I did was to go to the Louvre Museum.

3 I **had** [unstressed] trouble ordering **food** [stressed] because I **don't** [unstressed] speak any **French** [stressed].

4 **Once** [unstressed] I had **eaten** [stressed], I then **took** [unstressed] a tour bus to the Champs Elysées in **order to** [unstressed] do a bit of shopping.

5 When I **got** [unstressed] back on the tour bus and **started** [unstressed] taking pictures [stressed], I dropped my **camera** [stressed] over the side.

Extension

Ask students to read the sentences to their partner and practise stressing the appropriate words. Stronger classes could write their own sentences, involving stressed words, related to the unit topic.

Tell students to complete Exercise 08

Sample answers

1 This was rather exciting AS / SINCE / BECAUSE I had never done that before.

2 It took a long time to arrive AS / SINCE / BECAUSE I come from China.

3 It was a great experience ALTHOUGH next time I think I should study French.

4 I went to a restaurant AS / SINCE / BECAUSE I was pretty hungry around that time.

5 I went to the Champs Elysées to do a bit of shopping WHERE / AND I went on to buy as much as I could.

---

6 I then took a tour bus ONCE I had eaten.

7 I took the flight back to China AFTER everything was over.

8 I got back on the tour bus AND started taking pictures.

9 I started taking pictures BUT I dropped my camera over the side.

10 Once I had eaten, I THEN took a tour bus.

---

09 Exercise 09 discusses what happens at the end of a student's long turn. Focus students' attention on Tip 9, stating that at the end, they should try and summarise what they have said. After this summary, students will be asked follow-up questions, which will relate to what they have just spoken about.

Tell students to listen to the recording, which gives them some examples of follow-up questions. Tell students to complete questions 1-3.

Tapescript 41

A

Student:	… and it was a great experience. I think I'll always remember going to Tibet.
Examiner:	Do you generally enjoy visiting new places?
Student:	Yes, I would say I like to try new things … meet new people, so travelling is something that is very important to me.

B

Student:	… and it was a great experience. I think Paris is one of the best places on Earth for culture.
Examiner:	Would you like to visit Paris again?
Student:	Oh definitely. Maybe in ten years' time, I'd like to go back and see if anything had changed.
Examiner:	Is there anywhere else you would like to visit one day?
Student:	Yes, I've always thought about going to Rome. I mean I'm a big fan of the opera and love Italian food, so it's next on my list of destinations.

C

Student:	… and it was a great experience. London was one of the most interesting places I've ever been to.
Examiner:	Is there anything you didn't like about your holiday?
Student:	Maybe the weather … London isn't exactly famous for being a hot, sunny place to visit, but I didn't think the weather would be quite so bad as it was.
Examiner:	Would you recommend London to a friend?
Student:	Yes, definitely. But they would have to bring an umbrella! Everything else was wonderful though, I would definitely recommend it.

---

1 5

2 *Yes/No* questions and *Would* questions

3 The candidate took around 5–10 seconds to answer each question.

EXAM SKILLS

Tell students to complete this practice exam task, which covers Part 1 & 2 of the Speaking test (Exercises 10-12). Remind students they have one minute to prepare their answer for Part 2.

Tell students they will be monitored on the following:

their ability to answer all the points in the order they are presented in

the use of sequencing words to give their answers a clear structure

their use of sentence stress to convey meaning

their ability to respond to follow-up questions

READING

OUTCOMES

- skim a text to identify facts, opinions and theories
- match a fact, opinion or theory with a person
- recognise the use of *will* and *going to* future forms
- match sentence beginnings and endings about a passage.

OUTCOMES

The main aim of this unit is to help students to quickly identify facts, opinions and theories and to match these with a person. Elicit from students the difference between a fact, opinion and theory. The easiest way to do this is to ask students for an example of each.

Definition

Fact: something that you know is true, exists, or has happened.

For example:

England won the World Cup in 1966.

Opinion: a thought or belief about something or someone.

For example:

I think that Andy Murray will win Wimbledon again next year.

Theory: an idea or set of ideas that is intended to explain something.

For example:

According to all the sports experts, the new range of racing bikes will lead to new world speed records for at least the next two or three years

The unit also deals with two task types: matching features and matching sentence beginnings to sentence endings, relating to a reading passage. Students also learn to recognise and understand the use of the future forms, *will* and *going to*.

LEAD-IN

01 Tell students to read statements 1-3, and decide which is a fact, opinion or theory. Have them share their ideas with the class to ensure there is a consensus.

1 opinion	2 theory	3 fact

Elicit from students which words/phrases helped them identify which statement was a theory and which was an opinion.

Extension

In order to give students further practice, give them the following exercise:

Decide whether the following introductory phrases express an opinion or a theory:

Many scientists believe in…

In my view…

Several experiments have proved ….

I would argue that ….

I do not believe ……

02 In pairs, ask students to discuss statements 1 & 2 in Exercise 01. Go round and monitor the pair work and make a note of any good points to share with the class afterwards.

03 Draw students' attention to the information box (Tip 3), which highlights that, although matching features tasks are usually about a person, they can also be about a place, year or thing.

Exercise 03 is an example of this type of task and text. Elicit or feed the meaning of "entrepreneurs". Ask students if they know any entrepreneurs.

Definition

Entrepreneur: someone who starts their own business, especially when this involves risks.

Ask students if they recognise any of the entrepreneurs in the pictures.

04 Monitor the pair work and support where necessary. Encourage some pairs to feed back to the class and collate the main points on the board.

A Andrew Carnegie

One of the wealthiest businessmen of 19th century
Self-taught

1889 became owner of Carnegie Steel Corporation

Donated approx. $350 million to charities, foundations and universities

B Henry Ford

Founder of the Ford Motor Company

Made cars affordable to the masses

Introduced assembly line and conveyor belt – could make a car every 93 minutes

C Estée Lauder

Started her beauty company in 1946

First product was skin cream developed by uncle

Believes success due to high-quality products and excellent customer service

D Steve Jobs

Co-founder of Apple Computer with Steve Wozniak

Started company in 1976 at age of 21

Revolutionised the computer industry – iPod, iPhone, iPad, Mac

05 Elicit that the text is factual and ask students to provide sentences from the text, which supports this.

> factual

06 Elicit from students what is meant by key words (the important words which give the sentence meaning). Underline the key words in the first statement as a whole class.

> 1 fast – quickly, every 93 minutes
>   popular – the masses
> 2 family member – uncle
> 3 at home – family garage
> 4 first-rate –
>   looking after clients – customer service
> 5 gave … wealth away - donated

07 Tell students to find synonyms for the key words in the text. This exercise is useful, because as stated in Tip 7, the same words are rarely found in both the question and the text. Therefore, when approaching this type of task, it is useful for students to be aware of the synonyms used.

08 Exercise 08 is an example of a matching features task, and students have to match the statements in Exercise 06 to the correct person, A-D. As stated in Tip 8, students should base their answer solely on the information in the text and not on any prior knowledge they may have of the subject. Focus students' attention on the second tip for Exercise 08, which makes students aware that some of the options could be distractors. Elicit from students what a distractor is. The incorrect option in a multiple- choice task, designed to distract students from the correct answer.

> 1 B   2 C   3 D   4 C   5 A

09 Have student work in pairs or groups to decide the correct sequence. Then have students feed back to the class and try to reach a consensus

> 1 C   2 E   3 A   4 F   5 B   6 D

10 Tell students to read the title of the text in Exercise 10 and look at the pictures. What might these business ideas be? Trying to predict the content of a text by reading the title and looking at visual clues is a good habit for students to adopt.

11 Exercises 11-14 put into practice the steps in Exercise 09. Tell students to complete Exercises 11-14. As stated in *Tip 14*, remind students once again, to be careful of distractors.

> 2   The text is mainly opinion-based.

13

1 **Paragraph B:** Peter Diamandis, Jeffrey Jones
  Paragraph C: Peter Coker
  Paragraph D: Jason Matheny, Professor Post
  Paragraph F: Daniel Kluko

2 1 save lives
  2 harmful
  3 controlled using technology
  4 fulfil a worldwide need
  5 significant impact … existing business

3 1 save lives – search and rescue
  2 harmful – serious health problems
  3 controlled using technology – an app … will be able to handle
  4 fulfil a worldwide need – satisfy a growing global demand
  5 significant impact … existing business – mean the end of traditional

14

> 1 C   2 A   3 B   4 E   5 F

GRAMMAR FOCUS: FUTURE: WILL AND GOING TO

15 In this unit, the text in exercise 10, uses the future forms, will and going to. Understanding how these are used and how they differ, can have a significant impact on the meaning of a text. Tell student to complete Exercise 15, which clearly illustrates how they differ in meaning.

> 1 going to   2 both

16 Tell students to complete Exercise 16, which puts this information into practice.

> 1 will / are going to   2 is going   3 will

17 Another task type, which features in the reading exam is matching sentences. In this exercise students have to match sentence beginnings to their endings.

As a whole class, complete the first statement with one of the options, A-E.

Tell students to complete questions 2-5.

> 1 C   2 E   3 A   4 B   5 D

18 This exercise gives students some important advice about this task type. Tell students to read each statement and underline the key information.

> 1 questions, order
> 2 part of the … text
> 3 grammatically similar
> 4 Focus … sentence beginnings
> 5 similar words

Extension

To check learning, you could ask students to close their books and then quiz students on some of the important information.

- Do the questions test just a part of the text?

19 Matching sentence beginnings to their endings, will always relate to a reading passage in the exam. Tell students to read the sentence beginnings in Exercise 19, which relate to the text on page 90.

20 Tell students to scan the text and match each of these sentence beginnings to the section of the text they relate to. Check students remember the term scan (= to read a text quickly for specific information).

Match the first statement as a whole class, and make students aware that the sentence beginnings follow the order of the text (as stated in Tip 19).

i.e the section relating to statement 1, is likely to be found towards the beginning of the text.

1 A	2 C	3 D

21

1 e	2 a	3 d

EXAM SKILLS

Alternative

If you want to make this task more interactive and interesting for students, write these sentence endings and beginnings on separate pieces of paper and then ask students to physically match them together.

23

1 C	2 E	3 A	4 B	5 D

WRITING

OUTCOMES

- analyse an 'advantages and disadvantages' essay task
- plan your ideas and organise them into paragraphs
- use linkers to make your essay easy to read.

OUTCOMES

This lesson focuses on the, "advantages and disadvantages", essay task. This type of exercise features in Part 2 of the Writing exam. An "advantages and disadvantages" essay looks at both sides of the argument, students need to look at both sides of the argument and decide if the positives or benefits outweigh the negatives or drawbacks. Students will also look at how to organise this type of essays and how to make them easy to read. It is important that an essay is easy to read in order to have a positive impact on the reader or examiner. This unit will teach students how to plan and organise their ideas. Furthermore, it will also show students how these ideas can be successfully joined together, through the use of linkers.

Clarify what linkers are by writing some simple sentences on the board and asking students to join them:

I like coffee.	I love tea.
I love cake.	I hate biscuits.
I don't eat bread.	I want to lose weight.
I want to do well in the exam.	I am going to study hard.

Elicit from students examples of linkers, which will best join these sentences:

(and, but, because, therefore)

If appropriate, give a definition of linkers.

Definition

Linkers: words, which join one idea/sentence to the next.

LEAD-IN

As stated in the information section, in Part 2 of the Writing test, students could be asked to write an essay on the advantages and disadvantages of a particular topic.

Point out that students don't always do well in this type of essays, because they don't use appropriate structures or linkers.

Tell students to look at the photographs of people working in the country and in the city. In pairs, ask students to discuss questions 1 & 2.

In order to help students think of ideas for question 1, discuss a few examples as a whole class. Alternatively have students brainstorm in pairs and then share their ideas with the class.

Sample answers

Country

Advantages: more physical work, healthier, more enjoyable, less stressful

Disadvantages: paid less, less opportunity for promotion, difficult in bad weather

City

Advantages: higher pay, busy, exciting, lots of opportunities

Disadvantages: tiring, busy, difficult to get to work

As stated in *Tip 1*, this speaking exercise reflects the type of content needed in the writing answer. Students need to present both sides of the argument and then give their own opinion.

Exercises 02 & 03 focus on helping students' plan their answer effectively. Planning is particularly important in Part 2 as the essay should be approximately 250 words. As this answer needs to be fairly long therefore, it important students keep their answer relevant, structured and coherent, as highlighted in the information box.

Alternative

Suggest that students make notes of their discussion to get them used to preparing written answers. Students could work in pairs and groups to correct spelling and grammar. Encourage students to discuss the problems in 2 and see if they can add any others. For 3 get students to share their experiences in pairs and then collate them with the whole class on the board.

Draw students' attention to the information box, stating the importance of analysing the task carefully. Perhaps the most important aspect students need to realize about part 2, is that their answer needs to be relevant.

Advice

It is crucial for students to analyse the task carefully before attempting to answer it in order to ensure that they are answering the specific question being asked rather than a similar one they may have done before when practising.

Ask questions to focus on the importance of analysing the task. e.g.

Why should you analyse the task before writing? Discuss in pairs which of the following are valid reasons, then feed back to the class.

A To make sure your ideas are relevant.

B So you can change the topic if you can't answer the questions.

C To make sure you answer all parts of the questions.

D To be able to plan out the paragraphs you will need to answer the question fully.

All are valid reasons except B

04
1 **Task:** extent / agree/ disagree
   Topic: workplace after school / more beneficial / university

2 **Task:** advantages / disadvantages
   Topic: get a job / unpaid internships

3 **Task:** reasons, How ... tackled
   Topic: stress / major problem

05 Tell students to discuss their answers.

The second stage in the planning process is for students to brainstorm their ideas. As explained in the information section, brainstorming allows students to focus solely on their ideas, and not be worried by other aspects, such as grammar.

This section shows students two of the methods, which can be used to brainstorm mind maps, involving circular diagrams or linear plans, such as tables.

06 Tell students to brainstorm ideas for questions 1 & 2. They should use both methods and decide which one they feel most comfortable with.

Give students a maximum of 5/10 minutes to complete each plan as it's important that students should get used to writing down their ideas quickly.

1 Wearing a uniform

2 Big company

Advantages	Disadvantages
Meet more people	Less personal
More opportunities for promotion	Perhaps limited to one type of task

Once students have decided which ideas they are going to include in their essay, they just need to present them in a clear and structured way. This section gives students a possible structure for an advantages/ disadvantages essay.

07 Tell students to use the paragraph planner in Exercise 06 to structure one of the essays brainstormed in Exercise 07.

Alternative

Suggest that students could also structure their ideas kinaesthetically by using ideas written on slips of paper.

Check that students understand all the linkers in the box. In order to make their meaning clear, you could ask students to complete this table with the words from the box.

Cause & Effect	Addition	Time	Summary	Example	contrast
consequently	also	whilst	In conclusion	For example	however
therefore	furthermore				in contrast

You could also ask students to think of other examples for each column.

08
1 consequently   2 Furthermore / Also
3 therefore   4 For example   5 also
6 In contrast / However   7 Also / Furthermore
8 In conclusion   9 Whilst 10 however

09 Exercise 09 checks that students have understood and remembered some of the key points about this essay type. Tell students to complete Exercise 09 in pairs.

1 approximately ten minutes

2 mindmaps, linear plans, bulleted lists, etc.

3 your English

4 Yes, your answer must all be relevant.

5 No, because it is unlikely you will have an essay in the exam with exactly the same title.

6 a minimum of 250

7 yes

EXAM SKILLS

10 Remind or elicit from students their answers will be marked on the following:

relevancy

logical structure

use of cohesive devices

Then have students do the task under examination conditions without further support.

Alternative

As this lesson is focused on planning, you could also ask them to submit their plans for feedback prior to doing the written task. You could also grade the plans if appropriate. Make sure that students are fully aware that this will not be the case in the actual exam.

Sample answer

The way in which we work has changed a great deal in recent years.

Whilst some people still travel to their place of work each day, others have the option to work from home. This has all become possible since the birth of the internet and smartphones, which enable workers to be in constant contact with their colleagues and clients all over the world. There are both advantages and disadvantages to this new development.

They are definite advantages to people being allowed to work from home. The main advantage is that it gives workers more flexibility in their working life. This can be particularly useful for parents or people who live far from their workplace. Working from home is also more comfortable and you can take a break whenever needed.

Another advantage is that you have the possibility to work for companies in other countries, through the use of the internet. Therefore people can apply for jobs globally as well as locally.

On the other hand, working from home can also have its disadvantages. Travelling to work and working in an office with others can be a very sociable activity, which many people enjoy, especially if they live on their own. Without this social interaction many people might feel very lonely. Furthermore, many people may lack sufficient discipline to complete the work they need to do without colleagues around.

In conclusion therefore, there are clearly advantages and disadvantages to working from home. Perhaps the ideal arrangement would be to spend part of the working week in an office with colleagues, and part of the working week at home, with a certain amount of flexibility and comfort.

LISTENING

OUTCOMES

- use notes to follow a talk or lecture
- identify information needed to complete notes or sentences
- recognise the language of comparison and contrast to predict ideas in a talk.

OUTCOMES

In this lesson students will use notes to follow a talk or lecture. This context is common for sections 3 & 4 of the listening test, which are always set in either an educational or training context. The second outcome teaches students to complete notes or sentences, by identifying the relevant information; a common task in the listening. The third outcome shows students that they can use the skill of prediction to help them locate the correct answer, through recognising the language of comparison and contrast.

LEAD- IN

01 In order to generate interest in the unit topic, ask students to discuss the pictures in Exercise 01. What jobs are the people doing? Do you think they work for a company or for themselves? Try to elicit what students also know about different types of business in their own country and in the English-speaking world. Encourage students to talk about friends or family members, who work for themselves, have partnerships or businesses with a small number of employees. Get them to talk about others who work for bigger companies etc, and ask them to describe what sort of companies they are. Collate different ideas on the board. Encourage students to use dictionaries to clarify the three different types of business in the box: sole trader, partnership and limited liability company. Before playing the recording, tell students to underline the key words in the descriptions and make sure they understand their meaning.

Definition

Finance: money

Corporation: business

Tax: money that you have to pay to the government from what you earn or when you buy things

Shares: a part of a company

Income tax: tax that you have to pay on the money you earn

Much of the language may be new to students, so it might be necessary to play the recording more than once.

Alternative

If students need more help with this, give them a copy of the tapescript and ask them to underline the key words in each paragraph.

Tapescript 42

Dr Lethbridge: In last week's lecture I talked about employment and aspects related to it, including contracts, income tax and so on. However, people are increasingly looking at other forms of earning a living by working for themselves and being in greater control of their working lives. Today Dr Korpis and I are going to talk about three different ways in which people can work for themselves. They can set up a company, set up a partnership, or they can work as a sole trader. There are important legal and financial matters to take into consideration when choosing one of these structures as a way of doing business in the UK.

First, I just want to outline the main differences between these three types of business structure, which are to do with tax and registration. Regarding registration, those wanting to set up a limited liability company have to legally register the company with Companies House, the government department responsible for businesses. 'Limited liability' means that, if the business fails and the owners owe a lot of money, they only lose the money and goods which are in the business, and not their own personal money and goods. This is because the owners of the company are separate from the company itself. On the other hand, a sole trader doesn't need to set up a company; he or she can simply start working without any legal registration. A partnership can be limited or unlimited. An unlimited partnership is just like a sole trader, but with two or more partners. In this situation, each partner shares expenses and also income. A limited liability partnership, or *LLP* for short, is like a limited company, because it must be legally registered in the same way. So just to summarise: with limited liability companies and limited liability partnerships, the owners and the company are separate in legal terms, but with simple partnerships and sole traders, the business and the owner are not legally separate.

The other main difference is to do with money – both with finding money to start your business, and with paying tax. For example, it might be difficult to borrow money from the bank if you're a sole trader, but easier if you have a limited company, as banks trust companies more. Regarding tax, limited companies pay corporation tax, which, unlike income tax, is a tax on business profits, not personal earnings. This is more favourable for companies, as corporation tax is usually less than income tax. On the other hand, with sole traders and partnerships, whether simple partnerships or limited liability partnerships, the owners must pay income tax, which may be higher than corporation tax.

A limited liability company	B sole trader
C partnership	

Elicit from students which words/phrases helped them to find the correct answers.

As demonstrated in Exercise 01, listening out for key words, is essential for the note completion task.

02 Tell students to listen to a second lecturer talk about being a sole trader and ask students to correct the notes if necessary. Again, if needed, extra support can be given by playing the recording more than once, by stopping the recording at key points or by giving students a copy of the tapescript.

Tapescript 43

Dr Korpis: Thank you, Dr Lethbridge, for your introduction. I'd now like to move on to the details of each type of business structure and discuss the advantages and disadvantages of each, starting with the sole trader. This is simply a person who runs a business alone. On the practical side, there's no need to register with Companies House, which means the sole trader is not legally the same as a registered company. The trader can simply choose any name and start trading without paying any fees. There's no need to register an office, so the trader can even work from home. There are also no legal requirements to submit financial accounts to Companies House. As a result, this is the simplest and most straightforward way to start out in business and work for yourself. Another benefit of being a sole trader is that you are your own boss. You don't have to answer to anybody else, you make your own decisions and you don't have to share your earnings with a partner. However, it doesn't mean that you have to do everything alone. You can also employ or give contracts to other people to do work for you, though, of course, you need to be aware of regulations regarding employing others.

So these are the desirable aspects of being a sole trader but there are other matters which need careful consideration. When you're in employment, you are taxed at source, which means your employer takes your tax from your earnings every month and sends it to the tax office, so you don't need to worry about it. However, as a sole trader, you are self-employed, which means you are responsible for what you earn, what you spend and the tax that you must pay. This means you have to complete an annual tax return. This is a document which you send to the tax office once a year showing what you earn from your business and what you spend in running your business. On the positive side, you're only taxed on your earnings after expenses, such as transport, electricity, office equipment and so on. So, if you work from home, you can save tax by declaring some of your use of electricity as necessary for your business. Another consideration is that if you earn over a certain amount, you pay a higher rate of income tax, which is higher than the corporation tax rates that companies pay. You'll also have 'unlimited liability', which means that if you can't pay your business debts, you may lose your house and car to pay for them, as you are your business. Finally, many sole traders find it difficult to take holidays and breaks from the business and find that they spend far more time working than employed people.

The typical traders associated with this type of business structure are skilled manual workers, such as builders, plumbers and electricians, or professions in which people usually work alone, such as photographers and writers. However, increasingly these days, with the reduction in long-term employment and job security, sole traders are coming from other professions, such as computer programming and even teaching, especially tutoring. Certainly, being a sole trader is a very useful way of starting out in business by yourself.

A Correct

B Incorrect: sole traders may employ other people

C Incorrect: sole traders must pay tax every year, not every month

D Correct

E Correct

03 Exercises 03 & 04 focus on completion tasks, which specify how many words/numbers are needed to complete the missing information. It is very important that students keep to this word limit, otherwise they will lose marks.

Check students understand the words in the box, eliciting meanings or by having students check meanings in a dictionary.

Definition

Accounts: an official record of all the money a company or organization has received or paid

Contracts: a legal agreement between two people or organizations

Debts: an amount of money that you owe someone

Tapescript 44

Dr Lethbridge: Thank you, Dr Korpis. The next form of business structure that I would like to discuss is the 'partnership'. There are two kinds of partnership – a simple partnership and a limited liability partnership or 'LLP'. I'll talk about each of these in turn. Forming a simple partnership is straightforward, like becoming a sole trader, except that you have to agree to work with someone else. A partnership could be between a husband and wife, or two members of the

same family or close friends. For example, a couple might run a catering business, or two car mechanics might leave employed work to set up a partnership together repairing cars. One obvious advantage of this is that, if one partner is sick or on holiday, the other partner can carry on the business, and another is that it can be easier for a partnership to borrow money from a bank than it can for a sole trader. Of course, partners usually have an informal agreement to work together, but it's always better to have a formal arrangement to avoid disagreements. As with sole traders, each partner must be registered with the tax office as self-employed and must send in a tax return once a year. In addition, as the partnership is unlimited, all members are responsible for debt, so you and your partners may lose your personal possessions to pay debts if the business fails.

The other structure for a partnership is the 'limited liability partnership', or 'LLP'. This is similar to a simple partnership as the partners share the income and expenses and also have to pay their own taxes to the tax office, but there are important differences. On the one hand, sole traders and simple partnerships don't have to legally register their businesses. On the other hand, LLPs have to be legally registered with Companies House. This means that at least two of the members are legally responsible for the partnership. They have to make sure that they send accounts to Companies House, as well as to the tax office. They also need to send in an annual return, which is a document showing the name, address and members of the partnership and any changes. If they don't do this, they may go to prison, so it's important to understand exactly what setting up an LLP means.

So why should partners enter into a limited liability partnership? Usually, an LLP suits certain types of professionals who provide services, such as accountants, lawyers, consultants and financial service providers. Another reason may be that partners want to do business with larger organisations, who would prefer to give contracts to a registered company or partnership. In any event, an LLP offers the flexibility of being in a simple partnership, but also gives the partners protection so that they only lose the money that they have put into the partnership if it fails. However, if partners earn a lot of money, they will still pay more tax than the owner of a limited liability company pays.

1 borrow money	2 pay debts	3 accounts
4 contracts	5 tax	

Tapescript 45

Dr Korpis: Thank you, Dr Lethbridge. The last form of business I'd like to talk about is the limited liability company. The owners of a limited liability company are called 'members' or 'shareholders' as they own shares in the company. A 'share' is a divided-up unit or part of the company. All businesses run the risk of failing or going bankrupt. If a business goes bankrupt, it has to close because it owes money and is not able to pay the money back. As I mentioned before, setting up a limited liability company, like an LLP, means that if the company fails or goes bankrupt, the business owners lose only what they have put into the business and not their own personal goods and property. This is the idea of liability – how much a business owes in debt if it can no longer operate and has to close. For example, if a sole trader goes bankrupt, he or she may need to sell his or her own house and possessions in order to pay any debts, because the business is not separate from the owner. With LLPs and limited liability companies, the owners and the businesses are separate, so property and goods owned by the business can be sold to pay debts, but not property and goods personally owned by the members or company shareholders.

Just as with LLPs, limited liability companies (or 'limited companies' for short) must be legally registered with Companies House. This means they must have a registered address, where all the company documents and records must be kept. As with LLPs, accounts and annual returns must be submitted every year so that anyone can have a look at the company's finances before doing business with it. The level of administration is higher than with other business structures and you need to have a managing director and at least one shareholder.

In terms of paying tax, the company has to pay corporation tax on its profits, which is far less than income tax on large amounts, especially over around £50,000. However, you also have to pay income tax on any money you take as a salary from your company. As with the other business structures, the company tax assessment must be submitted to the tax office, but for corporation tax rather than income tax. The shareholders also have to submit their own personal tax assessments separately. As we've already mentioned, the company owners must also submit accounts to Companies House. This can all be quite complicated, so it's a good idea to get professional help and advice from an accountant. It's important to remember that running a limited company is more complex than being a sole trader, so it's important to do careful research and consider your situation before deciding which type of business to run. In any case, you could start as a sole trader and, if business is doing well, turn your business into a limited company at a later date.

04 Exercise 04 presents students with a slightly different completion task. This type of exercise asks students to complete statements, which summarise the information from the listening.

05 In this exercise, the recording is discussing the advantages and disadvantages of different business structures. The topic may be something that students are not familiar with, but by looking at the structures used they should be able to predict which word is needed. It is important to point out to students that in IELTS as a whole they may come across topics they are not familiar with, but the tasks will be structured in a way that they can use the knowledge that they already have to complete them successfully.

Tell students to look at the table of notes and ask them to predict answers 1-5, using the words from the box. Students may not exactly get the right answers, but at least they will have an idea of the kind of words they are listening out for.

Alternative

You may wish to write the options from the box on cards for students, so they can eliminate certain ones for each gap before making a choice.

Tapescript 46

Dr Lethbridge: So, let me summarise the differences and similarities between each business structure. On the one hand, it's fairly simple and inexpensive to set up as a sole trader. You don't have to worry about lots of administration and financial organisation, and you can keep total control of your business and decision-making. On the other hand, you may end up paying more in tax than you would as a limited company, you are personally responsible for your debts and losses and it might be more difficult to get valuable contracts if your business does not have limited liability.

With regard to partnerships, there are two kinds: simple partnerships and LLPs. In comparison with sole traders, partnerships have the benefit of more people to plan and make decisions. It's easier to take care of the business when one partner is not able to take an active part, and it can also be easier to borrow money than for a sole trader. On the negative side, liability is shared among the partners and having more than one owner can make things more complicated when there are disagreements, or if the business needs to be brought to a close. One other difference between sole traders and partnerships is that the partners need to trust each other. If a partnership has serious money problems, one partner may leave the other to deal with the debts. Clearly this is not a problem for sole traders. One similarity between partnerships and sole traders, though, is to do with tax. The sole trader must submit a yearly income tax assessment to the tax office. The same is true of partnerships, as members are treated individually for this purpose.

When we compare simple partnerships with LLPs, we can find various differences. For example, LLPs are legally required to submit their accounts and annual returns to Companies House. This is not something that is required for simple partnerships. Another difference is to do with debt. In an LLP, the partners' personal possessions and property are protected. In a simple partnership, however, like sole traders, the members are personally responsible for any business debts.

Finally, limited liability companies have two main advantages over simple partnerships and sole traders: this type of structure limits the financial liabilities of the owners to business losses and not personal losses, and it can save money, as corporation tax is generally lower than income tax. On the other hand, there are a lot more administrative and legal requirements. Company accounts and an annual return must be sent to Companies House. Similarly, there is a legal requirement to keep company records at the registered address.

1 the other hand	2 the negative side
3 the same is true	4 however 5 Similarly

EXAM SKILLS

Draw students' attention to Tip 6, reminding students that spelling accuracy is very important and they could lose marks if answers are spelt incorrectly.

Alternative

You could ask students to predict the answers before playing the recording. You would then be able to assess whether they were approaching the task in the correct way.

Tapescript 47

Dr Korpis: To conclude this lecture, I'd like to present three case studies to show the different structures in action. I'll present each case, briefly discuss the possibilities and recommend the most suitable structure.

First, there's the case of Sanjay and Tanya, a couple who want to set up a catering service delivering food to businesses. The idea is to take orders from businesses on a daily basis and prepare food for delivery during the business day. They aim to target businesses in their local area to begin with, and then further afield as they expand. Their plans include a website to display their daily international menus and to provide an online service for customers to order and check when the food will be delivered. Clearly, it's not suitable to be sole traders, but they could organise themselves as a partnership or a limited company. It depends partly on how much money they can raise and how many people they intend to employ to prepare and deliver the orders. It might be best for them to start as an LLP, so that they can get funding more easily than if they were a simple partnership. They could start small and build from there. They could hand out contracts to other companies for some of their services, particularly for the website and delivery, if they intend to prepare the food themselves. Alternatively, they could set up a limited liability company if they expect to grow quickly and want to keep every aspect of their business in-house, employing staff directly. However, I would say the LLP model would work better here – giving them more time to focus on growing the business, rather than dealing with a lot of administration from the start.

Melissa and Jane have an idea for a website design service. They both studied software engineering at university and so they are both well-skilled in their field. They have both worked as designers for major organisations, so they have a good understanding of what's involved in running such a business. Melissa has also taken a Master's degree in Business Administration, so she's confident about her skills as a businesswoman. They've managed to save over £3,000 to rent office space and £10,000 to buy equipment to run their business. The best option for them would be to register a limited company and start trading straight away as they have a good level of knowledge and experience which will benefit them. They don't intend to employ anyone immediately, but the option is there if they need to in the future. An alternative would be for them to start as a simple partnership and expand from there, seeing how their work grows and then maybe setting up a limited liability company in the future (or they could make their partnership a limited one). But if they have confidence in themselves, there's nothing to stop them setting up a limited company immediately.

Barry is a motorbike enthusiast with many years of experience riding bikes. He's been working for a courier company delivering letters and parcels for over five years now and thinks that he'd do better if he worked for himself. The courier company provided him with his work bike and took care of maintenance and repairs, so if he works for himself, he'll have to buy his own bike for work and take care of it himself. This isn't a problem for him as he has three bikes for his own use already. He knows that he can build up regular clients from his contacts, but he's not sure if working as a sole trader is the best thing for him, as he's never been self-employed before. Another possibility would be to set up a limited company with a family member. This person wouldn't take an active part in the business – they would be known as a 'sleeping partner'. Finally, he could also choose to work in a partnership with other riders who are thinking of leaving the company, but he's not sure if that arrangement would last. On balance, the best option for him would be to start off as a sole trader with his own work bike and do that for a year or two to see how well it went, and then make a decision about whether to set up a limited company in the future.

1 food, businesses	2 limited (liability)
3 £10,000, equipment	4 knowledge, experience
5 three / 3 (motor)bikes / own (motor)bikes	
6 sleeping partner	

After the exam have students listen to the recording again while reading the tapescript. Have them spend time analysing the text in pairs and then share their ideas with the class. Do students note any particular techniques used by the examiner, which will help them to do other listening activities more successfully?

SPEAKING

OUTCOMES

Draw students' attention to the outcomes of this unit, which focus on Part 2 of the speaking exam. In Part 2, students are given a task card and asked to speak for two minutes. Using the topic of business and work, students practise this task type and are given ways to expand their answer, in order to ensure they speak for the full amount of time.

This unit also equips students with a variety of expressions they can use to describe their wishes and intentions, which is a frequent requirement of the exam.

The third outcome, gives students practice with subordinate clauses. Students will need a good understanding of these, in order to expand on some of their points in Part 2. Try to elicit or feed examples of subordinate clauses.

Definition

Subordinate clause: in grammar a clause that cannot form a separate sentence but adds information to the main clause.

I would like to work in a factory, *which makes chocolate*. *(subordinate clause)*

The fourth outcome helps students to sound more natural when speaking, by encouraging the use of contractions.

Definition

Contraction: a short form of a word or group of words:

'Won't' is a contraction of 'will not'.

Ask students to work in pairs to produce a list of common contractions and then share the lists with the class.

LEAD-IN

01 Tell students to look at the pictures in Exercise 01 and describe what they see. Which job is represented in each?

Try to elicit how the people are feeling/look.

With stronger groups you might discuss job satisfaction. Why do they think these people look so positive? What things make people happy/unhappy in their work?

Ask students to match the pictures with the quotes. Elicit from students which key words helped them complete the matching exercise.

Example: children/ studies- teacher look after/ill- doctor

1 C	2 A	3 D	4 B

02 In this exercise, students practise talking about wishes and intentions, which they may have to do in the exam. Tell students to look at the expressions in the box. To check students have understood their meaning, ask them to label each expression as either a positive or negative comment.

Positive	Negative
I'd like to…	I'd probably hate
I hope that one day I can….	I'm not convinced that I'd…
I've always wanted to…	I'm not sure whether I'd
I wish that I could…	There is no way I'd…
I'd really love to	

Tell students to look at the photos and decide which job is represented in each picture.

Have pairs discuss the careers in the pictures, using the expressions from the box. You could ask stronger students to give reasons for their opinions as well.

' *I've always wanted to be in sales, because I really love meeting lots of different people.'*

03 Exercises 03 & 04 present more vocabulary associated with the topic of "work."

Tell students they are going to read four descriptions of jobs and they need to match each posting with a job title.

Alternative

With a weaker class, ask them to underline the key vocabulary in each posting and elicit the meaning of any unknown words. Tell students to match the posting to the job.

1 b	2 d	3 a	4 c

04 Many students will need support in completing the table. It might be helpful to complete the table for the first job with the whole class. Have students brainstorm and collate their ideas on the board. Then have students complete the rest of the task in pairs or small groups.

Finally ask students to discuss whether they would like to do each job. Check which is the most/least popular job.

Sample answers

Job	Qualifications / characteristics needed	Responsibilities	Pay / Salary / Wage	Benefits (e.g. promotion, retirement)
Model	Tall, good-looking	Showing off clothes, having pictures taken	Approx $50,000 per year	Free clothes, early retirement
Politician	Good talker, trustworthy	Spending public money, voting on social issues	$100,000 per year plus expenses	Free apartment and transport
Reporter	Good memory, fast typing skills	Looking for breaking news stories and reporting on them	$500 per story	Free camera, easy access to public figures

Sailor	Strong stomach, calmness in stormy waters	Navigation of the ship, ensuring safety of goods on board	$50,000 per year	Good travel opportunities

05 Exercises 05 & 06 give students examples of the kind of task cards they may encounter in Part 2 of the exam. They also give some useful advice and practice on how students can expand on each point.Tell students to read and answer in pairs the first task card, relating to the topic of jobs. Students have two minutes to speak about the task, one student should keep time, whilst the other speaks, and then change roles. Give students one minute to prepare and make notes, as is the case in the exam.

When students have finished practising this task, elicit from students if they struggled to talk for two minutes. Draw students' attention to Tip 5, giving advice on how to expand their answers, by giving examples or making comparisons.

Tell students to look at the question words and then match to their stem. These questions are examples of how this particular task can be expanded.

1 e	2 a	3 c	4 d	5 f	6 b

06 Tell students to look at the task card in Exercise 06, and then create 6 questions to accompany the task, as demonstrated in the previous exercise.

Sample answers

1 What kind of person are they?
2 Who else knows about this person?
3 When did this person become successful?
4 Where was this person successful?
5 How did they become successful?
6 Why did they succeed where others have failed?

Tell students to practise answering the task in pairs.

07 This exercise gives students more practice at speaking for two minutes.

It is important for students to develop a real sense of how long two minutes is.

08 Exercises 08 & 09 focus on two points of grammar, which are useful when completing this task type; subordinate clauses and contracting modal verbs.

Tell students to read the quotes in Exercise 08, demonstrating the use of subordinate clauses. Elicit the meaning of subordinate clauses, as outlined at the beginning of the lesson. Draw students' attention to Tip 8, highlighting the importance of subordinate clauses.

Once students have understood the use of the relative clauses (which, who, when, where) ask them to complete statements 1-5 with their own ideas. Complete the first statement as a whole class, to give students an example.

Sample answers

1 I once worked as a waiter, which was really hard work
2 I've often thought about becoming a singer, which might be very tough.
3 I've always been an admirer of my father, who is now a successful restaurant owner.
4 I remember how the music business used to be in the past, when the Internet wasn't around.
5 I would like to work in a museum one day, where I could spend all day in a quiet place

09 Elicit from students that the use of contractions makes the language sound more natural. Tell students this exercise focuses on the contraction of modal verbs.

Definition
Modal verbs: a verb, for example 'can', 'might', or 'must', that is used before another verb to show that something is possible, necessary, etc.

Elicit from students examples of modal verbs, e.g. will, would, can, could.

Tell students to complete Exercise 09, by listening to the difference between contracted and not contracted modal verbs.

Tapescript 48

1a I would love to work as a computer programmer.
1b I'd love to work as a computer programmer.
2a I would not like to be a pilot as I do not like heights.
2b I wouldn't like to be a pilot as I don't like heights.
3a I will apply for a position as a receptionist.
3b I'll apply for a position as a receptionist.
4a I will not look for a job straight away after graduation.
4b I won't look for a job straight away after graduation.
5a I should have taken a part-time job at university.
5b I should've taken a part-time job at university.
6a If I had studied harder, I could have got the job.
6b If I'd studied harder, I could've got the job.

10 Tell students to do Exercise 10 by completing each sentence and contracting the modal verbs. Do the first one or two sentences as a whole class and drill the pronunciation of the contracted forms, if necessary.

Sample answers

1 I'd love to be a tour guide.
2 I wouldn't like to be a vet, as I don't like seeing animals in pain.
3 I'll apply for a job as a finance manager.
4 I won't be looking for work as a teacher.
5 I should've studied harder at school.
6 If I'd got an 'A' in my exams, I could've gone to Harvard University.

EXAM SKILLS

11-12 Tell students to complete the practice exam tasks in Exercises 11 & 12.

Again, ask one student to keep time, whilst the other speaks (Part 2).

Tell students you will be looking for the following as you go round and monitor:

- their ability to express wishes and intentions in a variety of ways
- their ability to speak for a full two minutes, expanding where necessary (Part 2)
- their knowledge of vocabulary associated with the topic of business/work
- their use of subordinate clauses to expand on a topic
- their use of contractions, in order to sound more natural when speaking

READING

> ### OUTCOMES
>
> - approach *Yes / No / Not Given* questions
> - identify whether statements in questions match the writer's views
> - use *so, too, either* and *neither* to agree or disagree with someone
> - complete a summary with words from a box or words from a passage.

OUTCOMES

Focus students' attention on the unit topic of the natural environment. Elicit from students what is meant by natural environment (sea, land, air, in fact anything which is not man-made)

Ask students if they are interested in specific environmental topics. Have them work in pairs to brainstorm topics, issues and related vocabulary. This will help gauge their interest in the subject and generate some key vocabulary, which can subsequently be shared with the class.

This unit teaches students how to approach Yes/No/Not Given questions. Questions which test students' ability to match statements in the questions to the writer's views. It also gives students practice at the summary completion task type.

LEAD-IN

01 The words in Exercise 01 are common when dealing with texts on the environment. Have students check meanings in a dictionary if necessary. Tell students to match the words in the box with their definitions. Encourage stronger students to give examples of the use of some of the vocabulary or situations in which they have met them. Some students may be able to talk about of illegal poaching in Africa or give examples of animals that are in danger of extinction.

> 1 habitat 2 extinction 3 conservation 4 endangered
> 5 species 6 threaten 7 poach 8 captivity

Extension

If you have time and if appropriate, you may also want to drill the pronunciation of these words, as this topic is also common in the speaking exam.

Exercises 02, 03 and 04 discuss Yes/No/Not Given questions, a common task in the reading exam. The purpose of this task is to identify if the statements in the questions match the views or claims of the writer. Focus students' attention on Tip 2, which explains the difference between *a view* and *a claim*. Ask students to give their own examples of 'views' and 'claims'. (If appropriate with stronger groups, let them choose their own contexts for these.)

02 Tell students to read the short text in exercise 02 and answer the questions.

> 1 Yes 2 Not Given 3 No 4 Yes

> 1 involvement – contribution / make an impact – makes a difference
> 3 most people – the majority of [us]
> 4 do a great deal – go to great lengths

Make students aware that texts are not this short in the exam and that this exercise is just to give students the idea of the task type. Ask students to discuss in pairs the synonyms and other words and phrases that helped them find the answers, Have pairs share their findings with the class afterwards.

03 In order to help students tackle a longer text, Exercise 03 suggests a possible approach. Tell students to order the steps. If some students find this difficult, you could suggest they choose the first and last steps first, and then they decide on the middle stages.

Alternative

With weaker classes, write the steps on cards and ask students to work in small groups and put them into a logical sequence.

> a 4 b 7 c 5 d 3 e 1 f 6 g 2

04 Tell students to read the title of the text in Exercise 04.

Alternative

In order to personalise the topic and increase student involvement, you could ask:

Do you like visiting zoos? Why/why not?

What are the advantages/disadvantages of keeping wild animals in captivity?

Do you know of any 'famous' zoo animals?

How do you think zoos have changed in the last fifty years?

What kind of things do you predict the article will say?

Tell students to skim read the text and answer the questions, following the approach suggested in exercise 03. Before starting the task, draw students' attention to *Tip 4*, stating that the questions appear in the same order as the text.

> 1 Not Given 2 Not Given 3 No 4 Yes

GRAMMAR FOCUS: SO, TOO, EITHER AND NEITHER

05 Exercises 05 & 06 explore the use of, so, too, either and neither, phrases used to agree or disagree with someone. Understanding the use of these small words is important, as they can have a huge impact on the meaning of a sentence.

Tell students to complete exercises 05 & 06.

06
1. 'Me too.' / 'So do I.' / 'I do too.'
2. 'I wouldn't.'
3. 'Me too.' / 'So am I.' / 'I am too.'
4. 'Neither do I.' / 'Me neither.'

Alternative

If there is time, encourage students to work in pairs or small groups and do simple role plays involving the environmental topics.

Exercises 07 to 10 discuss summary completion tasks. As stated in the information box, there are two types of summary completion task. One provides a box with possible answers and the other requires an answer from the text.

07 In this exercise students have to choose from a list of words. Tell students to complete the summary.

When they have finished, draw their attention to Tip 7, stating that in order to confirm they have chosen the correct answers, they should read through the sentences to check they are also grammatically accurate. Encourage students to do peer correction and feedback the results whole class.

1 C 2 E 3 A 4 G

08 Exercise 08 draws students' attention to distractors. Feed or elicit from students the meaning of distractors. Ask stronger students to identify the best distractors in their view and justify their choice.

quickly – 3 animal – 2

09 Exercise 09 gives an example of a summary completion task, whereby students need to fill the gaps with a word from the text.

Tell students to complete Exercise 09 by skimming the text to understand the main ideas.

10 Draw students' attention to Tip 10, stating that before scanning the text for a word, they should decide what type of word they are looking for.

Example: Mountain gorillas are one of the most
1_____ species in the world.

Elicit from students that the type of word missing from the sentence above is an adjective. Then elicit how they know this? (follows "most"- superlative phrase)

Before asking students to scan the text for the word, ask them to predict the answer. (interesting, desired etc..)

1 endangered 2 habitats 3 poached 4 conservation

EXAM SKILLS

11 Tell students to complete the practice exam task in Exercise 11, using the skills and knowledge acquired throughout the lesson.

1 No 2 Yes 3 Not Given 4 No
1 E 2 F 3 B 4 J 5 G 6 K

Finally ask students to summarise in their own words the techniques and approaches learned in the lesson and agree three or four bullet points to guide them in the future.

WRITING

OUTCOMES

- avoid writing irrelevant ideas in an 'agree or disagree' essay
- express your ideas clearly in an essay
- write in an appropriate neutral/ formal style
- avoid repeating words and phrases.

OUTCOMES

The outcomes of this unit focus on Part 2 of the writing test, in which students may be asked to write an "agree or disagree" essay. This lesson explains how to keep essays relevant and how students can express their ideas clearly and focuses on the key components of a successful answer. It also teaches students how to write in an appropriate style and use a wide range of vocabulary in order to avoid repetition.

LEAD-IN

01 Ask students to discuss the questions in Exercise 01, introducing them to the topic of recycling/ saving energy a theme, which could feature in the exam. Encourage them to compare and contrast approaches and attitudes to the topic in different countries. Which countries in their experience are the best/worst at conservation?

02 Exercise 02 asks students to decide whether they agree, disagree or agree to a certain extent, with a set of statements concerning the environment. This is good practice for Part 2 of the writing exam, in which students are asked to provide their opinion in this way.

Alternative

Some students may find this exercise difficult, either because they are not used to expressing their opinion or because they do not know much about this topic. If this is the case, you could complete the exercise as a whole class and write some of the most relevant ideas on the board.

03 This exercise teaches students how to ensure that their essays for Part 2 are always relevant; a key requirement for this part of the test. Tell students to focus on the information box, which reminds them of the need to read the task carefully, underline key words and then spend time planning their answer. Write the task in Exercise 03 on the board and as a whole class underline the key words. (Some people believe … should be fined … do not recycle … what extent … agree … disagree)

Tell students to read the sample answer and then answer questions 2-4 in Exercise 03.

03

Another important aspect of the writing test is the use of the correct writing style in essays. The language used must be formal and academic. Students should not include therefore, any abbreviations, bullet points or slang/ colloquial language. Ask students to work with a partner and make a list of examples of common abbreviations and slang/colloquial language. Have pairs share the results of their deliberations with the class afterwards. Collate examples on the board.

Definition

Slang: informal language, often language that is only used by people who belong to a particular group

Abbreviation: a shorter form of a word or phrase, especially

Used in writing: A doctor is often called a 'GP', an abbreviation for 'general practitioner'.

Advice

Students should also be aware of the following when writing formally:

Do not use contractions (it's, I'm, his name's)

Generally, avoid phrasal verbs e.g. get away with, carry on

Avoid vague words e.g. nice, things

Don't use exclamation marks, dashes or etc.

04 Tell students to rewrite the sentences in Exercise 04, so they sound more formal.

Extension

If students need further practice at distinguishing between formal and informal language you could ask them to write short role plays in both styles. Present the dialogue below as an example to students.

A: Hiya, how are you doing? My name's Mary. I've come to do a bit of research on the environment, for something I need to write for school. Have you got any info for me?

B: Yes, we have lots of books on this.

A: That's awesome! How many books can I take away with me?

B: You can have a maximum of five.

In order to add a fun element to the exercise, students could then practise role playing in pairs.

Draw students' attention to *Tip 4*, stating that another way to sound more formal is to use the passive. Elicit some examples of the effective use of the passive, for example describing processes or when the person doing the action is unknown or not important.

Ask students to read the information box, stating that another way students can get a good score in the exam is by using a wide range of vocabulary and avoiding repetition.

05 This exercise demonstrates how repetition can be avoided. Tell students to complete the sample essay, using the words from the box.

Do the first question as a whole-class and elicit from students which word they are trying not to repeat (world)

EXAM SKILLS

06 Tell students to complete the timed exam task in Exercise 06. Inform students they will be marked on the following:

- the relevancy of the answer
- their ability to express their ideas clearly
- their use of a formal/academic style
- their range of vocabulary/ avoiding repetition

Another reason environmental issues are ignored is that people do not know enough about them. Although it is generally understood that recycling helps to save resources, this is perhaps the only step people take to help the situation. Most people have heard of global warming and pollution, but do not fully understand the implications. If they did, I am sure they would use their car less and try at all costs to save resources more.

Many people also believe that these environmental problems will not impact society for another fifty to one hundred years. Consequently, people feel these problems can be dealt with then by future generations.

Overall therefore, whilst there may be some people who are fully aware of the environmental problems facing the planet, the majority of the population still do not give them the attention they deserve.

After the exam ask students to recapitulate the main points in the lesson in their own words.

LISTENING

OUTCOMES

- complete a diagram showing a process
- answer multiple-choice questions
- understand the use of signposting words
- revise quantifiers with countable and uncountable nouns.

OUTCOMES

This unit discusses two task types from the listening test; completing a diagram showing a process and answering multiple choice questions.

This lesson also looks at the use of sign-posting words and phrases, as these are important when being asked to follow a lecture or talk, a possible requirement for Part 2 & 4 of the test.

Definition

Sign-posting: words and phrases give the listener an indication of where they are in a talk and/or what they are expected to hear next.

They might indicate, for example, how many points will be covered, give examples or provide, a summary.

Have students work in pairs to write a list of sign-posting words and phrases and then have pairs share their ideas with the class. (firstly, secondly, and then, after that, in the next part of the talk, finally, to conclude, in conclusion)

The fourth outcome revises the use of quantifiers with countable/ uncountable nouns. This is an aspect of grammar which many students often need practise with.

Definition

Quantifier: a word or group of words that is used before a noun to show an amount of that noun. For example the words 'many', 'some', and 'a lot of' are quantifiers.

Countable noun: a noun that has both plural and singular forms.

Uncountable noun: a noun that does not have a plural form and cannot be used with 'a' or 'one'. For example 'music' and 'furniture' are uncountable nouns.

Ask students to give examples of other uncountable words. (water, sugar, milk, food, metal etc.)

LEAD-IN

Tell students they are going to listen to a lecture about the environment and energy sources. Before playing the recording feed or elicit the meaning of renewable and non-renewable energy sources (A renewable form of energy can be produced as quickly as it is used/ non-renewable sources cannot be replaced once they have been used).

Ask students to explain in their own words what the energy sources in the box and in the table mean. They might be able to give examples of countries which rely heavily on each source. Ask them to look up words they don't know in a dictionary.

> **Alternative**
>
> Give students a copy of the definitions below and then ask them to work in pairs or groups to match the energy source to the definition.

Definition

Fracking: a method of getting oil or gas from the rock below the surface of the ground by making large cracks in it. Fracking is short for "hydraulic fracturing"

Petroleum: thick oil found under the Earth's surface which is used to produce petrol and other substances

Solar Power: electricity produced by using the energy from the sun

Wave power: power taken from the motion of sea waves

Hydroelectric power: using the force of water to create electricity

Coal: a hard, black substance that is dug from under the ground and burnt as fuel

Natural gas: a gas that is found under the ground and is used for cooking and heating

Tell students to listen to the lecture and complete the table with words from the box.

Tapescript 49

Lecturer: This week in environmental studies, we're going to look at the latest developments in the energy industry and how they might affect our lives in the future. As we've already seen, there are basically two types of energy source – renewable and non-renewable. As you no doubt remember, renewable sources are those which can be used again and again, while non-renewable sources can be used only once and then they're finished. Historically, coal has been the most-used form of non-renewable energy, but it has also been the most polluting. It's widely accepted that we need to use less of it to help protect the environment for the future. The oldest renewable source is wind power, which has been used for centuries to power windmills and other devices, and which has now been developed further, giving us wind turbines which produce electricity. Over the last 200 years or so, petroleum has become the most important non-renewable source, though natural gas is overtaking it as it's far cleaner and less polluting. Hydroelectric power has been in use for many years as a renewable resource, especially with dams on rivers and lakes, but these are expensive to create and maintain, and can affect the local environment in negative ways. More recently, there've been great developments in two renewable sources: solar power – that is, power produced directly from the sun, and wave power, which comes from the movement of waves at sea, but, of course, these are only effective in areas with a lot of sun or coastal areas. While there are clear benefits to expanding solar and wave power, one other source has become particularly significant and important, and that is fracking, which is a way of getting natural gas out of the ground. So, the main focus of today's lecture is on fracking and why there's been so much discussion and debate about it in the media.

Renewable sources: wave power, solar power
Non-renewable sources: fracking, petroleum

02 Exercise 02 discusses a listening task type in which students have to complete a diagram showing a process. Students need to listen to the recording and complete the missing labels.

Extension

Encourage stronger students to do the matching activity in 2 before they listen to the text. They can, perhaps, use previous knowledge to do one or two matches and then use visual clues to make educated guesses about the others. Then ask them to listen to the recording and confirm if their predictions were correct.

Tapescript 50

1   You can use this machine to make a hole in something. For example, you use a small one to make a hole in the wall to hang a picture, or a big one to make a hole in the ground.

2   This is a hole in the ground, which is dug in order to extract water, oil or gas.

3   This is a kind of rock deep in the ground that isn't very hard and is easy to break.

4   This is a narrow space, which appears inside rock when the rock breaks. The space can fill up with water or gas.

A 2   B 4   C 1   D 3

03 Try to elicit as much of the information below through guided questioning. Feed the information if students are not forthcoming. If necessary, get students to state the information in their own words to ensure they understand.

1   You should look at the whole diagram to get a general idea of the topic but your main focus should be on the missing words, thinking about what they might be.

2   You do not need to understand all the words. Your main focus should be on the missing words. The exam will not test your knowledge of difficult words, which might appear in the diagram. In this diagram, it is clear which part is above ground and which part is below ground, so you can get a good idea that a word you don't know refers to something under the ground. However, you don't need to worry about this as your focus should be on the missing words.

3   The large circle shows you some important information in more detail and focuses your attention on an important part of the process. The colours in the large circle help you understand how the process works as it progresses – in particular, how certain liquids flow in and out.

4   It starts at the well where certain materials go down into the ground and then turn to go along through one of the layers. Then something else comes out and goes back up to the well at the top.

5   The first and second words clearly refer to the layers. The third word clearly refers to something happening in the ground. The fourth word clearly refers to something that comes out of the ground. When you look at the diagram, focus on these words and listen for the sections where these parts of the process are discussed. Don't worry about other words that you might not understand.

04 Tapescript 51

Lecturer: So, what exactly is fracking? It's a way of getting gas out of the ground. Both oil and gas are found deep underground, so to get to them a well must be drilled. Normally, when a well is drilled into ground where there's gas, the natural pressure of the gas pushes it to the surface, where it can easily be taken away and stored. However, a lot of gas is found inside a type of rock called 'shale', where there is no natural pressure to push the gas out. If a well is drilled into shale, the gas will not come out by itself. It needs extra help. This is when fracking is an important way of getting the gas out. The fracking process works in this way: first, a well is drilled into the ground, through the water table (which is the natural level of fresh water). When the drill reaches the shale, which is where the gas is, it turns sideways through 90 degrees and continues horizontally through the shale. So, to put it simply, the drill goes down into the shale, where the gas is, and then turns to the side. Then, a mixture of water, sand and various chemicals are sent down into the well. The mixture creates pressure in the rock and the rock breaks. These small breaks in the rock are known as 'fissures', and these fissures release the gas from the shale. The pressure of the mixture causes the gas to rise to the surface, where it can be collected and stored.

2 shale	3 fissures	4 gas	

This section of the lesson discusses the use of quantifiers. An understanding of how to use quantifiers accurately is important, especially in this part of the test when they are frequently used.

Tell students to read the information box and then ask for examples of quantifiers and countable/uncountable, as outlined at the beginning of the lesson.

05 Tell students to work independently and complete Exercise 05, by choosing the correct quantifier. Then have them discuss their answers with a partner and finally feedback their joint decisions to the class.

1 Few	2 much	3 All	4 Some	5 a lot of

Feedback

For each question elicit from students why they choose their answer.

06 Tell students to complete Exercise 06 by listening to the recording. If appropriate, play the recording more than once, but make them aware that in the actual exam, they will only be given the opportunity to listen once.

1 a lot of	2 few	3 some
4 more	5 a little	6 fewer

Alternative

Have stronger students predict which words/phrases fit into the gaps before they listen to the recording. Afterwards ask them to say how many of their predictions were correct. Also elicit why they chose any correct predictions.

Tapescript 52

Lecturer: One interesting fact is that fracking isn't new. It's been used for many years around the world, mostly to get the last oil from old wells after the pressure's dropped. But the process has become much better known with the move to fracking for gas and the search for new fracking sites.

Take Canada, for example. Fracking has been used there to extract oil for over 50 years and gas for almost 40 years. More recently, a huge amount of shale gas has been found in many areas of the country and drilling companies are trying to get licences to drill in these areas. For example, in the western region of British Columbia, it's estimated that there are over seven trillion cubic metres of gas which can be extracted. However, most regions haven't allowed fracking to take place because of various environmental issues, which I'll talk about later.

In the USA, the production of shale gas now is around six times greater than it was ten years ago, with more and more licences being given to companies to drill. As a result, shale

gas now provides around a quarter of all gas used in the US, and the cost of gas is only about a third of the cost in Europe and a fifth of the cost in Japan. However, because the price has fallen so much, companies are reducing their production and exporting more.

As in the USA, production in Australia has grown massively. Although production in Australia was always lower than in the United States, it's over 20 times greater than it was ten years ago and now supplies a quarter of Australia's gas requirement. It's also helped Australia to become a major exporter of gas. Billions of dollars are being invested in gas exploration and Australia may well become the biggest exporter of gas over the next few years.

The situation in the UK, however, is quite different. The amount of shale gas in the UK has been estimated to be as high as 400 trillion cubic metres. Although fracking could well provide over 70,000 jobs and attract over £3 billion in investment, very little has been done to develop the industry in the UK. Some estimates say that gas bills could be 5% lower if shale gas is produced in large quantities. However, the main problem for fracking in the UK is the high level of population. While in the USA there are on average only 40 people per square kilometre, in the UK there are almost 250 people, so fracking in any area will affect far more people in the United Kingdom.

1 a lot of	2 few	3 some	4 more	5 a little	6 fewer

07 Tell students to complete the table using the words from the box in Exercise 06.

Used only with countable nouns: few, fewer, several, many, every

Used only with uncountable nouns: little, much, less

Used with both countable and uncountable nouns: all, [a] lot [of], more, some

08-15 Another task type students will encounter in the listening exam, is multiple-choice questions. As seen in the reading exam, some of the options given will be distractors, and students must be aware of this. Exercises 08-15 practise this task type and give students strategies in dealing with distractors.

Tapescript 53

Lecturer: As you've heard, in countries like Australia and the USA, fracking has been increasing because governments see many benefits for energy supply and their economies. I'd like to discuss these benefits now and then talk about the problems which people have raised about fracking. Well, although increased production of shale gas will make sure that there's always enough gas for people's energy needs and the production of electrical energy, the economic benefit to the consumer is usually seen as more significant. As the supply of shale gas grows, energy prices will come down and consumers will save a lot of money, according to supporters of fracking.

08

Correct answer: B … the economic benefit … more significant …; prices will come down … according to supporters of fracking. The question says 'those who are in favour of fracking' which refers to the supporters of fracking. The correct answer is 'lower energy bills', which is the same as saying prices will come down. The idea of 'main benefit' in the question is reflected by 'more significant' in the script.

Distractors: A is incorrect because although better energy supply is referred to, it is not referred to as the main benefit; C is incorrect because although electricity generation is also referred to, there is nothing to say it is increased generation

09

supporters of fracking; economic benefit; energy prices will come down

11 Tapescript 54

Lecturer: Another important economic consideration is the increase in economic activity and employment that results from the development of fracking wells. When a new area is developed, the local economy benefits, with increases in services to the fracking company. Furthermore, as with all industrial developments, employment opportunities increase, with most new workers recruited from the population in the surrounding area – although many workers from outside the area are also attracted by the new vacancies. Of course, companies often bring their own workers with them when they start a new well.

11

Question: fracking starts

A: local businesses … lose … employees

B: bring in …. most

C: more opportunities

Correct answer: C *the local economy benefits, with increases in services to the fracking company.* The question says *'it creates more opportunities for businesses in the area',* which is the same as saying the local economy benefits.

Distractors: A is incorrect because the script says 'with most new people recruited from the surrounding area' but it does not mention these people moving from other local businesses. B is incorrect because the script says 'companies often bring their own workers', but there is no reference to this being 'most of the workers'.

13 Tapescript 55

Lecturer: Apart from the economic benefits of fracking, its supporters claim that there are significant environmental benefits as well. First, although burning gas produces carbon dioxide, which is the main greenhouse gas causing global warming, the quantities that

it produces are far less than the quantities produced by burning coal and oil. Some people estimate that it produces up to 50% less than the other fuels. Burning coal and oil also produces sulphur and mercury, which can be very dangerous to health if breathed in. Another benefit of fracking is that it reduces the amount of water needed for gas production. There's evidence that gas production through fracking uses half the water needed for coal, and a tenth of the water needed for oil. One final benefit could be its use as a bridge to carbon-free energy. This means that, although gas produces carbon dioxide, if gas can replace oil and coal, then the production of carbon dioxide will slow down and the development of renewable sources of energy can take longer.

13

Sample answers

3

A: does not … chemicals … harmful

B: slightly less … coal … oil

C: much less water … coal … oil burning

4

A: less

B: more water … production … coal … oil

C: time … environmentally friendly

3 **Correct answer:** A

4 **Correct answer:** C

Tapescript 56

Lecturer: Despite the benefits of fracking, which its supporters claim, there are clearly various concerns connected with it. Some of these are real, but it's possible that they're not as well-founded as opponents of fracking would have us believe. So, what exactly are these concerns? Well, we can divide them into three categories: environmental concerns, health concerns, and economic concerns.

To begin with, let's look at the environmental concerns. The first, and possibly most significant environmental concern is that, despite producing lower levels of carbon dioxide, shale gas is still a cause of global warming and so it should not be used. In effect, it simply stops energy producers and governments focusing on the real need to develop renewable sources of energy. What's more, it's likely that, although countries, which produce shale gas will use less coal and oil, the use of coal and oil will still continue to increase in other places, so globally there will be little or no benefit to the environment.

Another environmental concern is pollution. If the production site is badly maintained, dangerous chemicals can get into water sources and rivers and contaminate the water. While there's some evidence of this happening at existing production sites, it isn't clear whether this problem happens everywhere, so more research is needed.

The last environmental concern connected with drilling is that of earthquakes. We're more familiar with earthquakes happening in certain areas of the world like Japan and China, but there's evidence that drilling can disturb the ground in the local area, causing it to move and shake, which in turn damages buildings. Usually, these movements aren't serious, but they can cause a lot of worry to the local population, so they need to be considered. In fact, very few of these ground movements have definitely been caused by drilling, and it might be that people are worried because of what they hear or read in the media rather than the actual reality of the situation.

Now I'd like to turn to the economic concerns. Opponents of fracking say that the economic benefits are not as great as its supporters claim. While there's clearly an increase in economic activity in the areas where fracking is carried out, as I discussed earlier, there are often negative effects on agriculture and farming in these areas and there's good evidence that house prices fall, because people aren't willing to move into areas where fracking is taking place or has taken place. Another economic concern is that gas production can be very high at the beginning of the fracking process, but it can drop quickly, down to as little as 10% in five years. This can result in more drilling and greater use of water, which increases the cost of getting the gas out of the ground. The other main economic problem is that the estimated amount of gas in the ground may not be anywhere near as high as fracking supporters claim, so investing huge amounts of money in new wells may not benefit the economy at all.

This brings me to the last major concern: health. Fracking can bring with it a pollution problem. If the well isn't deep enough – less than 600 metres – or if there are problems with drilling, the chemicals can leak into the drinking water supply and cause problems for the local population. There've even been reports of residents opening their water taps and seeing brown water and mud coming out. However, it's not only the water supply, which can be affected. Pollution can also be carried in the air to local towns and affect

people with existing medical problems, especially those with breathing difficulties. There've even been reports of more cases of cancer among people living near production sites, as well as among the workers themselves. Clearly, a lot more research needs to be done on the effects of fracking on health.

So to summarise, there are significant environmental, economic and health concerns connected with fracking, but we need to carry out a lot more research to see whether these concerns are real. Whether they're real or not, they're having an effect on the fracking industry right now. In many places around the world, local people have protested angrily when they've found out that fracking is planned in their area. These concerns have also led local, regional and national governments to announce that fracking won't start until they're quite sure that it's safe. This means that they'll prevent any activity connected with fracking until there's enough evidence to assure its safety, especially in areas with higher populations. In fact, in France, they've decided not to allow fracking anywhere in the country. We can see that the future is very uncertain, and that's what I'd now like to discuss.

14

1 **Correct answer: B** *although countries which produce shale gas … will still continue to increase … little or no benefit to the environment*

2 **Correct answer: A** *there is good evidence that house prices fall*

3 **Correct answer: A** *chemicals can enter the drinking water supply … residents … seeing brown water and mud coming out*

4 **Correct answer: B** *local, regional and national governments … fracking will not start until they are quite sure that it is safe … they will prevent any activity … enough evidence to assure its safety*

This section helps students follow a lecture or talk, a scenario they are likely to encounter in section two or four of the listening test, in which students will be given a monologue to listen to.

In order to help people follow a lecture/ talk, speakers often use signposting. Elicit the meaning of signposting, as outlined at the beginning of the lesson. Draw students' attention to the information box, which gives examples of signposting strategies.

16 Tell students to complete Exercise 16.

1 first (SE) 2 What's more (AD) 3 Secondly (SE) 4 last (SE)
5 Now (T) 6 While (C) 7 earlier (SE) 8 Clearly (AT)
9 summarise (SU) 10 that (T)

Tell students to focus their attention on *Tip 16*, outlining the importance of signposting.

EXAM SKILLS

17 Tell students to complete the practice exam task, using the skills and knowledge acquired throughout the lesson.

Tapescript 57

Lecturer: While fracking is being used around the world, we've seen that there are serious concerns about it. What's clear is that fracking isn't the answer to the growing worldwide need for energy as countries increase their consumption. Already, the amount of carbon dioxide in the atmosphere has reached 400 parts per million. This may not seem very high, but we have to remember that 200 years ago the level was around 280 parts per million, so it's increased by over a third since then. As a result, it's estimated that global temperatures have already increased by almost one degree Celsius. This increase changes the climate and affects the weather in many parts of the world. Many places, such as north-west Europe, are expected to become warmer and wetter and we've seen winter storms becoming worse in this region. Other places such as sub-Saharan Africa are expected to become hotter and drier, with deserts growing in area and seriously affecting farmland. Ice in the polar regions will melt and sea levels will rise, which will put coastal cities in greater danger of flooding.

Clearly, we need to reduce, and eventually stop using non-renewable resources, like coal, oil and gas. It may well be true that fracking can slow down global warming for a while and allow us to develop better renewable resources. However, these resources, like wind, wave and solar power, are currently far more expensive to develop than shale gas production. On top of that, they take a long time to develop and start paying for themselves. Consumers have to pay higher bills to help the development of cleaner sources, and energy companies don't want to lose customers by asking them to pay more. Consequently, it's important for international organisations like the United Nations and national governments to support the development of renewable resources. The problem here, of course, is that governments usually think of short-term answers to energy problems and not longer-term ones. They're afraid that if they reduce the production and use of gas and oil, their economies will do worse than other economies, so they don't want to take action to increase the use of renewable sources.

As I mentioned earlier, there are many people in different countries, like Canada, the UK and France, who don't support fracking, especially if it's going to take place near where they live. Environmental groups also oppose fracking, not just because they want to protect people living in areas where fracking is planned, but also because they see fracking as part of the old way of doing things, like burning coal, oil and gas and increasing global warming. They want to see continued action and are trying to persuade governments to develop wind, wave and solar power, as well as other renewable forms of energy, to fight global warming and ensure the supply of energy in the future. Certainly, coal, oil and gas will run out one day, and if we haven't developed other forms of renewable energy, we'll have serious problems with supplying energy to the growing world population, and the problems of fracking will seem relatively unimportant.

1 B	2 B	3 C	4 A	5 C

SPEAKING

OUTCOMES

- speak in detail about conservation and the environment
- recognise different functions in Speaking Part 3 questions
- express your opinions with the appropriate emotion.

OUTCOMES

Draw students' attention to the outcomes of this lesson, which prepare students to speak about the topic of conservation and the environment. This is a subject they may be asked to talk about in the exam, especially in Part 3 where they need to speak on more global issues.

This unit focuses mostly on Part 3 of the test, in which students are asked to express their opinions and they must also be able to recognise different functions for example comparing, assessing and explaining.

LEAD-IN

01 Focus students' attention on the two photographs. What do they show? Would you like to visit these places? Why/why not?

Tell students to discuss questions 1-3 in pairs. Go round and monitor the discussions and ask pairs who have had interesting discussions to feed back to the class.

This section of the lesson provides students with some useful vocabulary, which they may need when talking about the environment. Tell them to look at the words in the box and discuss the meaning of any unknown words. Drill the pronunciation of each word. *Drought* and *tsunamis* are words, which are likely to be tricky for students.

Elicit from students what type of natural disasters they have recently heard about in the news and also elicit any major disasters from the past. Ask if them to mention parts of the world where there are frequent natural disasters. Similarly get them to talk about any major incidents of man-made pollution they have read/heard about..

02 Tell students to complete the table using words from the box.

Natural disasters	Man-made pollution
volcanic eruptions	carbon monoxide
tsunamis	acid rain
drought	radiation leaks
hail	
thunderstorms	
tornados	

(floods, forest fires, landslides and sinkholes can go in either column)

03 This exercise asks students to put some of the words from Exercise 02 into a context. This will help to consolidate the new vocabulary,

Alternative

With a weaker class, you could first ask them to underline the key words in each statement and then match the key words to one of the words from the box.

Example

1. Humanity/blame/increase/emissions - carbon monoxide
2. Result/ homes/ burned down - forest fires

Sample answers

1 carbon monoxide 2 Forest fires
3 oil spills / radiation leaks 4 earthquakes / tsunamis
5 Acid rain 6 floods / landslides / sinkholes

04 This exercise personalizes the topic for students, by asking which environmental factors they have been affected by. Personalising the topic will make it easier for students to remember any new vocabulary. Be aware, however, that this could be potentially upsetting for some.

Tell students to discuss Exercise 04 in pairs. Go round and monitor the discussions and ask pairs who have had interesting/frightening/exciting experiences to feed back to the class.

Extension

You could extend this section further by asking students to discuss the following:

Why do you think certain areas are affected by these threats?

What can be done to prevent some of these problems?

05-06 Exercises 05 and 06 discuss words in English, which have silent letters when spoken.

It is important that students are aware of this when speaking, in order to achieve a good score in the exam.

Tell students to listen to the examples of this in Exercise 05 and then complete Exercise 06. Play the recording twice if needed.

Tapescript 58

scenic

business

Tapescript 59

1 calendar

2 foreigner

3 should

4 guest

5 autumn

6 honest

7 light

8 doubt

9 castle

10 yoghurt

06

1 calendar	2 foreigner	3 should	4 guest
5 autumn	6 honest	7 light	8 doubt
9 castle	10 yoghurt		

Extension

Tell students to look at the words in Exercise 02 and underline the silent letters. Ask stronger students to give other examples of words with silent letters.

Exercises 07 to 11 focus on Part 2 of the test, when students have the opportunity to write notes before answering the task. It is important that students make the most of this time and this section shows them how to do this. Encourage students to share their notes and write some on the board to cue a class discussion.

07 Tell students to read the task cards in Exercise 07 and then discuss the questions in Exercise 08 with a partner.

08

1 A: 'What makes it beautiful' and 'why this place is famous' require more information

B: 'What you remember most' and 'whether you would like to visit the place again' require more information

2 A: Where that place is – name of place

What kind of place it is – nouns (e.g. coast, mountain, lake, etc.)

What makes it beautiful – adjectives (e.g. unusual, breathtaking, etc.)

Why this place is famous in your country – reasons (e.g. in poems, travel guides, etc.)

B: When you visited this place – date

What kind of scenic features the place had – nouns (e.g. mountains, lakes)

What you remember most about the place – memory (e.g. sounds, sights, etc.)

Explain whether you would like to visit the place again – reasons (e.g. show it to someone else)

3

Number of examples required:

A: What kind of place it is – 1

What makes it beautiful – 2 or 3

Why this place is famous – 1 or 2

B: Scenic features – 2 or 3

What you remember most about the place – 1 or 2

Whether you would like to visit again – 1 or 2

4

Tenses required

A

Where that place is –present

What kind of place it is – present

What makes it beautiful – present

Explain why this place is famous – present

B

When you visited this place – past simple

What kind of scenic features the place had – past simple / past continuous

What you remember most about the place – present

Whether you would like to visit the place again – present conditional

Tell students to complete Exercises 09 & 10. Remind students they only have one minute to write their notes, so using a stopwatch is advisable. (Tip 9)

11 Exercise 11 demonstrates to students that their notes should be brief in order to make the most of the time limit. Tell students to complete Exercise 11.

> The second set of notes would be easiest to write in just 60 seconds.

12 This section of the lesson helps students to identify different functions, such as describing, explaining and comparing. Throughout the exam students will be asked to respond to several different functions, so it is important students are aware of what they are being asked to do.

Tell students to read questions 1-5 and match each one to a function from the box.

> 1 predict 2 suggest 3 compare 4 assess 5 explain

Extension

Elicit from students which words helped them identify the correct function.

1. will happen- predict
2. what can… do- suggest
3. any difference between- compare
4. have… done enough- assess
5. why- explain

Students could then write five of their own sentences, related to the topic of the unit expressing these functions, for example:

How will our environment have changed in fifty years?

What can we do to save our environment?

13 Exercise 13 focuses on Part 3 of the Speaking test, which asks students about society as a whole, rather than the student's personal experiences, as stated in Tip 13.

Tell students to read the sample answer to part 3 and complete with the appropriate function. Complete the first gap as a whole class.

> 1 compare 2 explain 3 compare 4 assess 5 explain
> 6 predict 7 compare 8 suggest 9 assess

Exercises 14, 15 and 16 teach students how to express their opinions, a requirement of Part 3. Exercise 14 discusses how a student's level of certainty in their opinion can be expressed by using certain words.

Tell students to complete the table using the words from the box.

14

Certain	Careful
certainly	likely
indeed	perhaps
surely	maybe
clearly	unlikely
no doubt	almost
will	might
of course	occasionally
definitely	seemingly

Extension

In pairs tell students to practise using these words in sentences, for example:

• I am unlikely to go out this evening.

• I will definitely pass my exam

With weaker students, do this activity as a whole class.

15 As stated in Exercise 15, it is important that students are prepared to have an opinion on any topic.

Tell students to complete Exercise 15.

Statement	Agree	Disagree
That's true.	✓	
1 That's right.	✓	
2 I'm not sure about that.		✓
3 That's also how I feel about it.	✓	
4 I have to side with you on that one.	✓	
5 Me neither.	✓	
6 That's incorrect.		✓
7 I beg to differ.		✓
8 You might have a point there.	✓	
9 I'm afraid I don't share that point of view		✓

16 Tell students to discuss the statements in Exercise 16, using the example phrases in 15.

EXAM SKILLS

In this sample exam task, students are given the opportunity to practise all three parts of the test.

Tell students to practise exercises 17, 18 and 19 in pairs. As one student speaks the other should keep time.

As you monitor, tell students you will be looking for the following:

- their ability to speak in detail about conservation and the environment.
- their ability to understand and respond appropriately to the function being asked of them.
- their ability to express their opinions with emotion.

Encourage some strong pairs to demonstrate their discussions to the whole class if appropriate. If the atmosphere in the class is very positive you might also invite peer assessment using the criteria above.

READING

OUTCOMES

- skim a text to locate information quickly
- understand a text in order to label a flow-chart, diagram or technical drawing
- use modals of obligation (*should, have to* and *must*) correctly.

OUTCOMES

Draw students' attention to the unit topic: education systems. Ask students to discuss what is meant by this (e.g. primary school, secondary school, college, university), what do students think of the education system in their own country. This is a topic which students could be presented with in any part of the exam. This unit will introduce important vocabulary, which may be needed to understand written texts on the subject. Tell students that this particular lesson focuses on university life.

Focus students' attention on the outcomes of the lesson. The first aim is to teach students to skim a text to locate the answers quickly, a key skill needed for the reading, as time is often the most challenging factor. The second aim is to teach students how to label a flow-chart, diagram or technical drawing by understanding a text. Elicit from students that the purpose of a flow-chart is to describe a process.

The final aim considers the use of modals of obligation. It is important that students are familiar with these, as their use can have a significant impact on the meaning of a sentence.

E.g. You must complete this module.- obligatory

You should complete this module.- optional

LEAD-IN

01 Exercise 01 gives students important vocabulary needed to read about the unit topic. Allow students to use dictionaries if needed.

Extension

As a warm-up, in order to generate interest in the topic, you could ask students to discuss the following:

Would you like to go to university? Where? What would you like to study?

Have you been to university? (give details)

How do you think/ know it differs from school?

01-02 Tell students to complete Exercises 01 & 02 by matching the words in bold with their definitions.

02

1 lecture	2 enrol	3 fund
4 assignment	5 campus	6 faculty
7 Master's degree	8 undergraduate	9 Bachelor's degree
10 postgraduate		

As a follow-up for consolidation ask students to work in pairs and ask each other questions about the vocabulary without looking at heir answers. In a later lesson you could make this a competitive class activity in the form of a quiz.

Completing a flow chart is one of the tasks students may be asked to do in the Reading exam. As stated in Tip 3, it isn't necessary for students to understand every word in the diagram or chart. Instead they should practise focusing on the key words and phrases.

03 Tell students to read the flow-chart in Exercise 03, and underline the key words and phrases.

E.g. Step 1- once, chosen, apply, university place.

04 Exercise 04 teaches students how to interpret a flow-chart. If students remember this list of questions and apply it to any flow-chart in the exam, they are less likely to panic.

1	how to apply to an Australian university as an international student.
2	choosing a university and enrolling / applying for a student visa / booking your flight and accommodation

1 adverb	2 noun	3 noun	4 adjective

05 Tell students to read the short text in Exercise 05 and complete the flow chart using just one word from the passage. Draw students' attention to both tips, stating that the answers do not always come in the same order as the text and that numbers/ hyphenated words count as one word in the exam.

1 directly	2 admission	3 funds	4 new

Alternative

In order to give students more help with this exercise, you could first ask them to underline the key words in each section/ paragraph. Students could also then decide which section relates to which step. In this instance, the answers do follow the order of the text. E.g. gap 1- paragraph 1/ gap 2,3, 4- paragraph 2.

06 This exercise shows students how to double-check they have chosen the correct answer.

07 This exercise gives students an example of a chart completion task. Elicit from students what the chart shows.

It illustrates a weekly timetable / schedule.

08 Tell students to complete the chart using no more than two words from the text. If needed, ask students to first employ the strategy given in Exercise 05. (underlining key words and matching sections to parts of the chart)

1 Lecture	2 Private study	3 Lecture
4 Football (training)	5 Tutorial	

GRAMMAR FOCUS: MODAL VERBS OF OBLIGATION: SHOULD, HAVE TO AND MUST

09 Exercises 09, 10 & 11 offer the opportunity to practise the use of modal verbs of obligation. These are important for students to understand as their meaning can have a significant impact on the meaning of a sentence.

09

1 c

2 a, b

3 b

4 a: I don't have to attend / I needn't attend
b: You don't have to have a great deal … / You needn't have a great deal …   c: You mustn't / You don't have to / You needn't / You shouldn't choose

5 a: I had to attend …   b: You had to have …
c: You should have chosen something you would enjoy / you would have enjoyed

10

1 must   2 don't have to / needn't   3 should / ought to

4 must not / mustn't

11

1 a – This expresses a rule and therefore something which is not allowed.

2 b – This expresses a rule and therefore something which is not allowed.

3 a – This expresses an idea which is optional.

12 This section of the lesson helps students to locate the answers quickly. Elicit from students why this is important. (Time is a challenging factor in the reading exam.)

As stated in Tip 12, students should identify which reading tasks they can tackle quickly, in order to allow more time for other tasks which take longer.

13-14 Tell students to study the diagram. What does it represent? (a campus map) Tell students to skim read the text and answer questions 13 & 14, which help students locate the answers quickly.

13

1 [University] library   2 Gym

3 Careers centre   4 [Main] reception

14

1 No, just the last two paragraphs

2 *main student facilities* (indicating where the information is) and prepositions (e.g *in front of, behind*)

Make students aware of Tip 13, advising students not to panic, if the diagram is difficult to understand at first. Diagrams are often scientific or technical in nature and students must be aware of this.

15 This exercise gives students an example of a technical diagram.

Alternative

In order to generate more interest in the exercise you could firstly ask students to discuss the following in pairs;

What does the picture show?

What was it used for?

Have you ever used one?

Why was it replaced by the computer?

Have them share their answers with the class afterwards.

Tell students to complete Exercise 15, making a note of Tip 15, which states that spelling accuracy is important. Also remind students, that it is not important that they recognise all the technical terms they are presented with, as these are explained in the text.

2 Lever   3 Type hammer   4 Ribbon   5 Carriage

As stated in the previous exercise, it is not necessary for students to recognise technical/scientific terms, but they are required to be able to understand explanations. This section therefore, discusses the way in which these explanations may be presented to students, using either a footnote, explanation in a text or explanation given through context.

16-18 Tell students to complete Exercises 16 to 18, which give students an example of each of these modes of explanation.

16

lever: footnote

ribbon: explanation in the text

carriage return lever: explanation given by surrounding context

17

1 a explanation in the text   b explanation in the text
c explanation given by surrounding context
d footnote

18

1 Hard drive   2 Input 3 LCD screen

EXAM SKILLS

19 Tell students to complete this exercise, using the skills and knowledge acquired from the lesson.

1 Professional   2 Honours
3 Full-time   4 Doctoral degree

WRITING

OUTCOMES

- generate ideas about a topic and express your opinion clearly
- organise your essay in a logical order
- proofread your writing effectively.

OUTCOMES

Focus students' attention on the outcomes of this lesson, which deal with Part 2 of the Writing. The first aim is to teach students, how to generate ideas and express their opinion clearly, which are the key requirements of this task.

The second aim focuses on structure, and helps students order their essay in a way, which will be easily understood by the examiner.

The third aim, practises proof-reading skills and reminds students that they need to check their essays carefully, once they have finished writing.

LEAD-IN

In Part 2 of the writing test, students are required to give their opinion. In preparation for this task type, it is a good idea for them to practise discussing different topics or perhaps having debates with classmates or friends. Elicit the meaning of debate (discussion or argument about a subject, e.g. *a political debate*)

01 Tell students to complete Exercise 01 using the expressions in the box.

This activity provides a lot of scope for extended discussions. There are several different topics, so depending on time available you might find it useful to allocate one or two questions to different pairs. Go round the class and monitor and support the discussions. Make a note of pairs who are generating a lot of useful language and give them the opportunity to perform in front of the class, if they are willing. Encourage students to give feedback to their peers after the pairwork.

02 It is important that students realize that only some of the expressions in Exercise 01 can be used in written English. Tell students to complete Exercise 02 individually and then agree the expressions whole class.

> For me, To my mind, Personally, I think

This section of the lesson teaches students how to express their ideas clearly, by structuring their essays well.

03 Tell students to complete Exercise 03 by allocating statements 1-9 to the introduction, main body or conclusion. If students need support with this, tell them to allocate the obvious ones first and then tackle the rest.

E.g. Introduction- introduce the topic-summary of your main ideas, conclusion.

> **Introduction:** 5, 6, 7, 9
> **Main body:** 2, 3, 4
> **Conclusion:** 1, 8

04 This exercise demonstrates how this suggested structure can be put into practice.

Alternative

With a weaker class, first ask students to assign each paragraph to one or more of the statements in Exercise 03.

> 1 D   2 E   3 A   4 C   5 B

Draw students' attention to Tip 4, stating that in order to achieve a good score, they must express their opinion at different points throughout their essay.

This final section of the lesson focuses on teaching students to check their work. As stated in the information section, it is easy for them to make silly errors, especially under exam conditions. Discuss with students how long they currently spend checking the aspects mentioned in the information box (spelling, grammar etc.).

05 Tell students to read the sample answer in Exercise 05 and correct the mistakes. There are 19 in total and cover all the aspects mentioned in the information section.

Alternative

Have students do the correction activity in groups. To facilitate this, enlarge a copy of the sample answer and ask students to use the following correction code:

P- punctuation

G- Grammar

SP- Spelling

After completion of the task, have groups swap answers and check that they agree with the corrections other students have made.

Using a marking code is also useful when you mark their essays, as it tells students what type of error they have made, but still leaves them to correct it themselves.

> **Nowadays**, many parents are choosing to home-schoo**ling their** children rather than sending them to a private or state school. There **are** perhaps many reasons for this, but I believe the main reason is that many schools are not seen as safe any more. In some areas, schools can be very violent and fighting is a common problem**.** I do not believe that home-schooling is always more beneficial to the student than state school, but in some cases it can be. In the following essay, I **will** discuss this idea further.
>
> If you are lucky enough to be able to attend a good school, with only minor **discipline** problems**,** then I think attending a state school is better for you than being educated **at** home. **S**chool is more than just learning about different subjects, it is also a place **where** you can meet new friends and learn to socialise. School also gives you the opportunity to join teams and clubs. **S**ubjects are also taught by people who have been trained in that particular area**.**

If however, this is not the case, and you have to attend a school with poor **discipline** or somewhere you feel very unhappy, then home-schooling could be more beneficial. It is better to learn in a comfortable **environment**, where you feel safe than in **a** disruptive one. **I**n order for home-schooling to be **successful** however, your teacher needs to be **knowledgeable** and follow a set **curriculum**.

To summarise therefore, home-schooling is more beneficial if the child is in a situation which is making them very unhappy.

EXAM SKILLS

06 Tell students to complete this timed exam task using the skills and knowledge acquired during the lesson. As stated in Tip 6, remind students that the neater their handwriting, the easier it is for the examiner to read.

Tell students you will be looking for the following:

Clear expression of ideas

Overall accuracy

Well structured essay

Clear handwriting

Try and use the error code suggested to mark their essays. You may also need the following:

WW- wrong word	M- missing word	RW- try re-writing
WO- word order	?- Not clear	R- register

Sample answer

The majority of students start their degree in the same year as finishing school or college. Some students, however, choose to take a year out before starting university. In my opinion, this is a very good idea if the time is used wisely in order to gain new skills or knowledge. In the following essay, I will discuss this idea further.

It is very important that, when a gap year is taken, the time is not wasted but used productively. It would not look very impressive to a future employer if the time was simply used to take a break. This does not mean to say that a gap year should not be enjoyed.

Many people choose to go travelling during their gap year. This can be very beneficial to the individual as it exposes them to new ideas and cultures. It can also mean that they are able to learn a new language. Other students decide to gain work experience during this year. This can be particularly useful, especially if connected to their chosen area of study. often, students who have worked before attending university appreciate their course more, as they are able to understand the relevance of what is being taught.

Overall, therefore, as discussed in this essay, there can be several benefits to taking a gap year. It is very important, however, that this time is used wisely and not wasted. This means that the year needs to be planned carefully in advance to get the most from the experience.

Alternative

If you want to add a fun element to this exam task or give students extra support, ask them to have a debate on the topic first- either as a whole class or in pairs. Have students collate key vocabulary and phrases on the board. This would give them a range of ideas for the content of their essay.

LISTENING

OUTCOMES

- listen to understand a description
- complete a chart, diagram or sentences based on a talk or dialogue
- use notes to follow what a speaker is saying.

OUTCOMES

Draw students' attention to the outcomes of the lesson. In this unit students will learn about three task types; chart completion, diagram completion and sentence completion. In the exam, students could be asked to complete one of these by listening to an academic lecture or dialogue. This lesson will teach students how to follow both of these and identify key elements.

LEAD-IN

01 Tell students to look at the pictures and the table in Exercise 01. In order to introduce students to the topic of the recording, ask them to discuss what age is associated with different types of schools in the UK. Students could start by discussing the places in the photos: (nursery school & sixth-form college)

Extension

Students could also compare and contrast the school system in their own country with the one in the UK. What are the similarities/ differences?

Tell students to listen to the short conversations and write 1-7 next to each type of education. Draw their attention to the example. For a weaker class, play the recording more than once and/or stop after each conversation.

Alternative

Play the recording in sections and ask students to listen to each conversation separately and write down the key words. They then discuss these words with a partner before completing the first column of the table.

Tapescript 60
Conversation 1

A: I'm sorry to hear that you didn't get the grades to get into university. What are you going to do now?

B: I'm not sure. I can take my exams again at the local college, but I'm not sure if I want to do that. Maybe I'll take a vocational course there instead to learn the skills for a particular job, like accountancy or business studies. At least if I pass that, I can go straight into work.

Conversation 2

A: So how's Jenny settling down? It's always difficult when they start school. My son, Timmy, took weeks to get used to being away from me all day.

B: Oh, she's fine. She loves it, especially learning to write. She doesn't miss me at all. I'm the one with the problem. I really miss her being at home all day. But after all, it's the law – she has to go!

Conversation 3

A: I've found this evening course in photography at my local centre. It's two evenings a week and only costs £150 for the term. You've always been interested in photography as a hobby. Why don't you come too?

B: Oh, I did that course last year. It's really good. I'm planning to take a course on setting up a website, so that I can display all my photos. It does seem strange, though, to be learning something new again after so many years!

Conversation 4

A: I think it's really useful for them to start early. I know it can be expensive, but it's worth it because they already know what it's like to be with others in a class when they start school.

B: That's true. In my case, it's not just the benefits of socialising with other children, it also means I can go back to work. It's a pity I can't get a free place for my son – though I don't have to pay very much, thank goodness.

Conversation 5

A: Well, my daughter is off tomorrow to start her degree course – a whole new adventure in a new city. I'm nervous, but she's really thrilled about it. There's a week for the new students – it's called freshers' week – when they find out what they need to know, join clubs and get used to being away from home, and then the course starts the week after.

B: Well, don't worry. I'm sure she'll be fine. After all, she's 18 now and they all have to make their own way in the world sometime.

Conversation 6

A: I'm a bit worried about my son. He's not doing very well. The thing is he needs to understand that it's not like his last school, when he did everything in the same class. He has to make sure he knows his timetable and gets to the right classroom on time. He keeps getting to class late and not doing his homework.

B: Don't worry. It often takes time for them to adjust to the idea of having more responsibility. I'm sure he'll do better when he settles down.

Conversation 7

A: My son passed all his GCSE exams and wants to go to university in two years' time. We can't decide whether he should continue at his school or go to that new college near our house. What do you think?

B: Well, the college has taken the best kids from the local schools since it opened two years ago and almost all of them have passed their A levels and gone on to university, so I think it's really good. Also, it makes them feel more grown-up when they go there.

02 There is a lot of written information for students to become familiar with before they listen to the recording. With weaker groups you could adopt a kinaesthetic approach and provide groups with the texts on cut-up slips of paper and ask students to label each with a type of school before they listen to the recording.

01–02

Nursery: 4, E
Primary school: 2, F
Secondary school: 6, D
Sixth form college: 7, G
Further education: 1, C
University: 5, A
Adult education: 3, B

03 Tell students to read the table carefully and then complete the task, by choosing from the words in Italics. Give students the first example and make sure they understand the meaning of *italics*. As stated in the information section, the *ages* mentioned will help students follow the lecture. With weaker groups you might do the reading in pairs followed by feedback to the whole class. This section of the lesson shows students how to tackle a chart/diagram completion task. Draw students' attention to *Tip 3*, stating that before completing this task type, students should first study the diagram or chart carefully, and predict the type of information which is missing.

Tapescript 61

Lecturer: The British education system is not the same everywhere in the UK. Scotland has its own system, and while Northern Ireland has the same basic system as England and Wales, there are some differences. Because of this, I'm going to focus mainly on England and Wales.

The system in England and Wales is divided into three main levels: primary, secondary and tertiary. In the first part of my lecture, I'll talk about the primary and secondary levels up to the age of 16, and in the second part I'll discuss the options between 16 and 18. Then, finally, I'll talk about tertiary, or 'higher' level education.

As in most similar countries, education at school is compulsory between the ages of five and 16. Pupils can leave school at 16 but they must stay in an approved learning environment until the age of 18. This can be full-time education, a job or volunteering combined with part-time study, or an apprenticeship, sometimes called a 'traineeship'. Before the age of five, children *can* attend nursery, though they don't *have to* attend any educational institution at all before the age of five. However, when they reach the age of four, they usually start school in an early class called 'Reception', which helps them to adjust to regular schooling.

Primary school runs from the ages of five to 11. The first part of primary school, between the ages of five and seven, is traditionally known as 'infant school' and this is where children learn to manipulate numbers, read and write. Traditional infant schools offer an informal education using child-centered techniques. The second part of primary school, from seven to 11, is known as 'junior school'. The education system has undergone various changes in the last 30 years, most notably with the National Curriculum, which was put in place in 1988 to specify a set of core main subjects that all school pupils have to study. These subjects have to be assessed at four key stages up to the age of 16. At certain stages, the children take exams known as 'Standard Assessment Tests', or 'SATS'. These tests are designed to check the pupils' progress against the national standards, as well as to provide teachers and parents with an assessment of their school's performance.

Key Stage 1 assessment comes at the age of seven, when the pupils do their first 'Teacher Assessments'. Key Stage 2 comes at the age of 11, when the pupils are ready to leave primary school. Although teachers assess their pupils' progress throughout primary school, at the end of Key Stage 2, unlike in Key Stage 1, pupils have to take 'Standard Assessment Tests'. Key Stage 3 is reached after the first three years in secondary school, when the pupils are 14. However, this time, the students are assessed directly by the teachers and not by sitting national tests. These assessments help teachers, students and parents to decide which subjects the students should choose to prepare for Key Stage 4, when they take exams which will help decide their future career choices. Unlike SATS, these assessments, known as 'General Certificate of Secondary Education' exams, or 'GCSEs', are not primarily designed to assess progress or give schools an official statement of their performance, but to provide students with their own personal qualifications.

The National Curriculum defined a set of compulsory subjects. These are subjects which the law requires all students to study. There are also some subjects which pupils and students have to study at different stages. For example, Modern Foreign Languages start in primary school, and continue up to Key Stage 3, after which they're optional. In secondary school, students take Citizenship from Key Stage 3. When they enter Key Stage 4, pupils are allowed

to make more choices. For example, all learners have to take History and Design and Technology up to the age of 14, but then they can choose whether to continue them or not.

1 Reception	2 Infant	3 Junior
4 Standard Assessment Tests		5 Teacher Assessments
6 General Certificates of Secondary Education		
7 Modern Foreign Languages		

04 This exercise requires students to do a diagram completion task. Tell students to listen to the lecture and complete the gaps using only one or two words.

As stated in the previous exercise, remind students to study the diagram carefully before attempting to complete the task. Play the recording more than once if needed.

Alternative

In pairs, ask students to predict the missing information, before you play the recording.

Tapescript 62

Lecturer: Now I'd like to turn to educational opportunities between the ages of 16 and 18. There are various choices open to pupils of this age. The first thing to decide is whether to start work or to continue studying full-time. Of course, starting work means going straight into employment, although young people aged between 16 and 18 will still need either to study part-time, as well as doing their job, or to join an apprenticeship or traineeship scheme.

For those who want to continue studying full-time, there are two paths: academic and vocational. Academic qualifications, mainly Advanced level exams, known as 'A levels', are taken by students aiming for university study. Vocational qualifications, such as those offered by the Business and Technology Education Council (or 'BTEC' for short), prepare pupils for a specific profession, such as engineering or computing. Most of those who wish to continue academic studies will go to the sixth form in their school or a specialist sixth form college. Alternatively, they can study A levels at a further education college, also known as an 'FE' college. Either of these routes will take students to university. On the other hand, those who wish to study a vocational qualification will typically go to a Further Education college, and, after qualifying, will be ready for employment.

There are other options for those who want to start work at 16. Since 2015, young people between the ages of 16 and 18 must continue to learn in a specified learning environment, in addition to working for an employer. The first option is to work for an employer and study part-time for a vocational qualification, such as a National Vocational Qualification (or NVQ for short). The second is to apply for an apprenticeship or traineeship. With apprenticeships, young people get to work with experienced staff and gain job-related skills. They earn a wage, although this is typically less than a 'regular' employee, and get to continue studying part-time – usually one day a week. They study towards a qualification related to the job they are doing and their apprenticeship can last anywhere between one and four years. Almost always, they are offered a permanent job by the same employer at the end of their apprenticeship.

1 Academic	2 Further education / FE	3 University
4 Employment	5 Apprenticeship	

05 This task requires students to listen to a text and then complete sentences by choosing the correct word. With weaker groups have students read the sentences in pairs and ask them to say what they are about whole class. Get them to highlight the words they have to choose from each time. With some very weak students you may need to clarify the meaning of some of the choices (What is provisional/conditional?).

Tapescript 63

Mr Green: So, Amanda, you want me to help you with your application. Let's have a look at the UCAS website. Do you know what 'UCAS' stands for, by the way? It's the University and Colleges Admissions Service. Have you set up an account with them yet?

Amanda: Yes. I did it last week, but I haven't completed my application. One thing I need to know is how many universities can I apply to?

Mr Green: Well, first of all, you need to see how many offer the course you want. Remember, you'll want to choose the universities, which have the best reputation, but you need to have some kind of back-up in case you don't get into your first choice. What are you studying?

Amanda: I'm doing A levels in Biology, Chemistry and Psychology, so I'm thinking of taking Biochemistry.

Mr Green: OK. Well, there are seven good choices I could give you. Apart from Oxford and Cambridge, Imperial College in London is very good, and York is also a good possibility and easier to get into.

Amanda: OK. I don't think I'll get into Oxford or Cambridge, so I can include York and Imperial College.

Mr Green: OK. I think you should go for those two, plus three others, because the maximum number that you can put on your application is five. How about Durham, Sheffield and Exeter?

Amanda: OK, I'll look at those. Another thing I'm not sure about is how to make a good assessment of myself and my skills and abilities. I've always found that difficult.

Mr Green: You mean your 'personal statement'? Well, just be honest. I can help you phrase it so that it reads well, but you need to note down what you want to include. If you can do that by Friday, we can write it up together.

Amanda: That's great! Thanks.

Mr Green: Well, that's what I'm here for – to give you the advice that you need. After you've completed your application, I can add the reference and your predicted grades before sending it to UCAS.

Amanda: Great! After we send it in, what happens next?

Mr Green: Well, UCAS processes your application and sends it on to each university that you've chosen. Then the universities assess it and decide whether to make you an offer. Remember that your predicted grades are only provisional, which means they are not confirmed until you get your actual results, so you need to pass the exams to actually get those grades. Usually any offer from a university will be a conditional offer. That means they can't give you a definite offer because it depends on your final grades. Then, when your exam results come through, they get sent to the school here and the universities.

Amanda: Do I have to contact the universities to ask them about my application?

Mr Green: No. They'll contact UCAS about their offer. If you meet the predicted grades, they'll usually confirm the original offer, but if not, they don't tend to renew it or change it.

Amanda: Oh, I hope that doesn't happen. But if it does, what can I do?

Mr Green: Well, if you don't get a place at any of your chosen universities, you can take a year off and try reapplying next year. Alternatively, you can try to get a place through 'clearing'. This is a way universities fill remaining places on their courses and it's a second chance for students to get into another university if they didn't succeed with any of their chosen ones. It's a sort of safety net, but I hope it doesn't come to that.

Amanda: Well, thanks for your help. I'll complete my application and then come and see you on Friday.

Mr Green: Glad to help, Amanda. See you then.

1 five	2 statement	3 reference
4 conditional	5 confirm	6 clearing

06 As demonstrated in the previous exercise, it is very important that students are able to follow a conversation and they are not confused all the extra information. Tell students to listen to this conversation and choose the correct set of notes for 1-5. Simplify the task for weaker students by focusing their attention on the choice of possible answers each time.

Tapescript 64

Dr Harris: Hi, Terry. Come in. What can I do for you?

Terry: Hi, Dr Harris. Well, I just wanted to check on some information about the course, as it's all new to me.

Dr Harris: Of course. What do you need to know?

Terry: Well, first of all, I'm not sure exactly what a seminar is for. We never had them at school. I know it's to discuss things together, but is it more than that?

Dr Harris: Well, yes, you're right, it is really. You see, at university we typically have lectures, you know, with about 100 or 200 students in the lecture theatre together. It's a one-way form of learning. The lecturer sets out the topic and discusses it and you take notes. Then you need to review your notes following the lecture and also do some extra reading.

Terry: And where does the seminar fit in?

Dr Harris: It could come at any time once you've had some time to think about the lecture. When you attend the seminar, you should have some of your own ideas to discuss with the other students, usually up to ten of you. It allows you to discuss the topic, exchange ideas and prepare for your assignments.

Terry: OK, thanks. And what about tutorials? Are they like seminars?

Dr Harris: Well, usually we try to space them out over the term, so that we can have a chance to check on your progress and how well you're doing with your assignments. It often depends on when your tutor is available, and at times that might mean you have three weeks between tutorials. Normally every term you should have one at the beginning, then usually another four, spaced out depending on your programme, and one before the holiday. So that works out about one every two weeks.

Terry: Right. And what about assessment? How many exams do we have to do?

Dr Harris: Well, that varies from course to course, but generally we focus on continuous assessment more than exams, though exams are, of course, very important too. We tend to assess you over the first two years through your assignments, which is over half of your overall assessment, usually 60%, and then most of your exams will come in the final year.

Terry: OK, I'm happy with that. I get really nervous before exams. And talking about assignments, how long should they be?

Dr Harris: On all undergraduate courses, students tend to write about 3,000 words or so, but it varies depending on the question. However, there's a minimum of 2,000, and while there's no upper limit, you should be careful that you don't write

too much as a lot of that might not be relevant to the question.

Terry: So I should aim for between two and three thousand as a rule … there's one last thing I wanted to check about assignments, and that's references. How many do we need generally?

Dr Harris: Well, as your course is international finance, you have to use banking, finance and news sources as well as academic sources. Ideally, you should have around ten references for each assignment to show that you've read widely, but we expect a minimum of five sources which are academic journals and books. From the other sources, we'd generally expect three to be used.

Terry: OK, thank you Dr Harris. That's cleared up a lot of things for me.

Dr Harris: Glad to be of help, Terry. See you next week.

1 a	2 b	3 a	4 a	5 b

EXAM SKILLS

07 This sample exam task practises sentence completion. Tell students to complete questions 1-5 with no more than two words. Suggest that students should read the sentences carefully and try to predict possible answers before they listen.

Tapescript 65

Dr Ross: So, Jessica, congratulations! You got a first class degree. I always knew you could manage it. What are your plans now?

Jessica: Thank you! I couldn't have done it without all your help. Well, I'm not sure. I'm still thinking about the possibilities. I'm not sure if I want to teach or go into research, or even find a position in a company, perhaps.

Dr Ross: Well, anyone with a degree in Chemistry will always be in high demand. Have you thought about teaching?

Jessica: Yes, but don't you need a degree in education to do that?

Dr Ross: Well, many teachers do that, but, of course, you have to be sure that you want to teach before starting your degree course. In your case though, your main route into teaching would be to do a Postgraduate Certificate in Education. That's another year of study, and you'll learn everything you need to know about teaching, while also getting teaching practice in your subject at local schools. You could study that here if you want.

Jessica: That sounds like a good idea. I'll think about it, but I feel I have more studying to do in chemistry before I think about teaching it.

Dr Ross: Then you could always take a Master of Science degree. That will allow you to specialise in a particular area of chemistry, but if you want to

Jessica: Yes, I see. Actually, I've often thought of doing a research degree.

Dr Ross: That would be a very good idea, but remember that it will take you at least three years to complete that. It would probably be better to do a Master's degree first and then transfer onto a PhD course. It also costs a lot, and you may need to fund yourself while you're studying. Have you thought of going straight into work?

Jessica: Yes, I have, but I'm not sure if that's the best choice for me.

Dr Ross: Well, you could try doing a company internship for a few months. A company internship is a chance to work in a company without actually being an employee, but possibly with some pay. It'll give you a chance to develop your career and also learn more about your subject specialisation in a commercial environment. After that, you may well get a good position in the company. We have some good commercial contacts for internships here.

Jessica: That might be the best option, but I wouldn't earn much to begin with, would I?

Dr Ross: No, you wouldn't. You could try getting a permanent job now if you want. There's a graduate fair here in the city every year, as well as in other cities around the country. You'll have the chance to meet all the leading companies in the sector and discuss opportunities with them.

Jessica: It's worth considering. Well, I have a lot to think about. Can I meet you again next week?

Dr Ross: Of course. Just send me an email and let me know when would be a good time.

1 Postgraduate Certificate	2 Master …Science
3 research degree	4 company internship
5 graduate fair	

SPEAKING

OUTCOMES

- speak in detail about education
- consider reasons, causes and effects for different Speaking Part 3 situations
- make suggestions or recommendations.

OUTCOMES

Draw students' attention to the aims of this unit. The overall focus of this lesson is to teach them how to speak in detail about the topic of education; a subject which can arise in any part of the exam.

The second and third aims of this unit deal with Part 3 of the Speaking, when students could be asked to discuss some or all, of the following: reasons, causes/effects, suggestions and recommendations. In order to make clear to students the meaning of each, write the following on the board and ask them to label each one.

I could help you with your homework, if you are having trouble. (suggestion)

I don't have my homework because the dog ate it. (reason)

If you don't attend your classes, you won't pass the exam. (cause/effect)

You should read this book. It will really help with your essay. (recommendation)

LEAD-IN

01 Tell students to discuss questions 1-4 with a partner. This activity provides a lot of scope for extended discussions. There are four different questions, so depending on time available you might find it useful to allocate one or two questions to different pairs. Go round the class and monitor and support the discussions. Make a note of pairs who are generating a lot of useful language and give them the opportunity to perform in front of the class, if they are willing. Encourage students to give feedback to their peers after the pair work.

Alternative

As a whole class collect feedback on questions 2 and 4.

Exercises 02 & 03 introduce some useful vocabulary on the topic of education.

02 Tell students to look at the words in the box and describe their meaning to a partner. With a weaker class, encourage students to look up unknown words in a dictionary and discuss the meaning as a whole class.

Tell students to complete the sentences 1-5 using words from the box.

1 teachers, discipline	2 tests, grades
3 academic, private tutors	4 curriculum, essays
5 technical, graduation	

03 Tell students to complete Exercise 03 using their own ideas and words from the box.

It may be useful to give students a short example first.

Draw students' attention to Tip 3, stating that education is a common topic in IELTS and may feature in Parts 1, 2 or 3 of the Speaking.

04 Exercises 04 & 05 give students practice at expanding their answers, by providing reasons for their opinions. This is particularly useful for Part 3 of the test, when students need to speak at length about a topic.

In pairs, tell students to read the opinions in Exercise 04 and then brainstorm reasons to support these ideas. Choose one of these statements to provide an example on the board.

e.g. 1. technology is making education more stressful.

ideas: sometimes it does not work / people become too reliant on it / students can use it to cheat / it costs a lot of money

Draw students' attention to Tip 4, stating that in order to speak at length on any given topic, they must have a wide vocabulary.

05 Exercises 06 & 07 discuss cause and effect. Elicit or feed the meaning of this, as outlined at the beginning of the lesson. In Speaking Part 3 students may well be asked to talk about cause and effect, in relation to a particular topic.

06 Tell students to read the problems described in the table and complete the causes column.

Sample answers

Problem	Causes
a Parents have to spend a lot of money on private education.	1 Because students are under a lot of pressure to get good grades. 2 As schools do not cover all of the subjects in depth. 3 Because our society is very competitive.
b Students do not have enough free time to socialise.	1 Due to the fact that they have to study from morning until night. 2 Because they have to prepare for their exams. 3 As our parents force them to use their free time to study.
c Many students have reported that they are unhappy with studying English.	1 As they have to spend a lot of time memorising lists of vocabulary. 2 Because it is considered as more important than their native language. 3 Due to the fact that it is difficult to learn a foreign language quickly.

07 Tell students to change partners and then focus on a different table, completing the effects column.

Sample answers

Cause	Effect
a Because students are under a lot of pressure to get good grades	1 Parents have to spend a lot of money on private education. 2 Their teachers are very strict. 3 They finish studying at 11 pm.

b Due to the fact that we have to study from morning until night	1 Stedents do not have enough free time to socialise. 2 They spend a lot of time sleeping in lessons. 3 Many students suffer from poor health.
c As they have to spend a lot of time memorising vocabulary	1 Many students have reported that they are unhappy with studying English. 2 Students struggle to make real conversation in English. 3 Students feel like they do not make much progress in their studies.

08 In Speaking Part 3, students are often asked to make suggestions or recommendations. In order to do so, they need to have a good understanding of modal verbs. Elicit or feed the difference between should, must & have to and then have students consolidate their understanding by completing Exercise 08 individually or in pairs. Ask students to give further examples if needed.

Sample answers
1 spend more money on teacher training
2 get to know their students' learning styles
3 try some extra-curricular activities
4 work together
5 quickly change its education system

Exercises 09, 10 and 11 give students practice at using all of the following: modals of obligation, providing reasons, explaining causes/ effects and giving suggestions. They provide all of the key language needed to participate successfully in Part 3 of the Speaking. Encourage a strong student organise the feedback to the class and the selection of the final ten items. Afterwards have students reflect on the performance of their group and the performance of others.

12-13 Tell students to look at the information section, giving examples of some contractions. Tell students to complete Exercises 12 & 13.

12

1 She'd	2 it's	3 I'll

Tapescript 66

1 I'd suggest going to bed earlier or you won't be able to remember what you've learnt.

2 We mustn't push young people into studying too hard, or they'll drop out of school.

3 That's not the right solution. Instead, we should've banned homework for pupils some time ago.

EXAM SKILLS

14 In Exercises 14 & 15, students will have the opportunity to speak at length about the topic of education. Tell student to complete Exercise 14. Remind them, that they have one minute to prepare the answer.

Their answers should display the following:

a clear structure

a good use of vocabulary

correct use of contractions and modals of obligation

15 Tell students to listen to the recording and make a note of any reasons, causes, effects or suggestions that are given.

Tapescript 67

Examiner: In your opinion, what is the effect of private tutoring on education?

Student: I think we have an education system where those who have lots of money do better than those who haven't, because many students can't afford private tutors. The tutors teach things at a higher level than the school curriculum, so many students see regular school as a waste of time. That's not really fair, so the government should change the law to limit the cost of private tutoring, so that it's more equal for everybody.

Examiner: Is private tutoring more important today than it was in the past?

Student: Well, I think that private tutoring is certainly more important now than in the past. I mean, in the past we only had tutors for English lessons as it was hard to find people who spoke English well enough to teach conversation in schools. But now we have tutors for everything, even tutors who teach three-year-olds how to pass interviews. Perhaps things have gone a bit too far now.

Examiner: What more can governments do to reduce the need for private tutoring?

Student: I think that governments must make changes to the curriculum so that schools cover all the subjects that are usually taught by private tutors, like English conversation, art, music and other things. If we can get these subjects taught more in schools, then students might not need to go to private tutors to learn them.

Examiner: How can we encourage more parents to teach their children at home?

Student: I know that parents are very busy, but they at least have free time at the weekend. This doesn't mean that they should spend their weekends making their children memorise lists of vocabulary, but perhaps if parents make time to do things like drawing pictures, reading, or listening to music, then children will not need to go to private tutors for those sorts of thing.

Sample answers

1 people with money do better; students think school waste of time; should limit cost of tutoring
2 more important now; tutors for three-year-olds
3 change curriculum to cover all subjects
4 do things like drawing, reading, listening to music

After students have listened to the recording, ask them to answer the questions with their own ideas.

UNIT/08: FESTIVALS AND TRADITIONS

READING

> ### OUTCOMES
>
> - find factual information in a text to decide if a statement is *True*, *False* or *Not Given*
> - practise identifying *Not Given* questions
> - recognise and use the first and second conditional correctly.

OUTCOMES

Draw students' attention to the first two aims of this unit, which deal with True, False or Not Given questions. For this task type, students need to read a factual text and then decide if the statements given are True, False or Not Given. Particular focus is then given to Not Given questions, as these statements are often the hardest to identify.

The third aim focuses on the recognition and use of the first and second conditional. It is important students recognise their use as they can have an important impact on the meaning of a sentence. Write the following sentences on the board:

1. If I had the money, I would celebrate my birthday on the beach. (2nd cond.)

2. If I have the money, I will celebrate my birthday on the beach. (1st cond.)

Ask students which conditional is being used in each statement?

What is the difference in meaning between the two sentences? (1- unlikely 2- more likely)

LEAD-IN

01 Tell students to skim read the three short texts, which describe some of the most interesting festivals in the world. In order to check understanding, ask students to describe the main points of each festival.

02 Tell students to complete exercise in pairs. Go round and monitor the discussions and offer support if required. Make a note of good ideas/use of language and feedback to the class. Also, feedback anonymously on any common errors.

> **Alternative**
>
> Read through the first text as a whole class and discuss the questions in Exercise 02. Students then divide into pairs and each read one of the remaining texts. Students then re tell what they have read to their partner and they both discuss the questions in Exercise 02.

03 Exercises 03-08 discuss True/False/Not Given questions, a common feature in the Reading. As stated in the information section, this task type is similar to Yes/No/Not

Given questions, but instead of being opinion-based these questions relate only to factual information. Make sure students know the difference between these two types.

Tell students to complete exercise 03, by choosing True/False or Not Given.

The texts will not be as short as this in the exam, but this exercise will give students a clear idea of the task type. Draw students' attention to tip 3, which states that the questions are in the same order as the text.

03

1 False	2 True	3 Not Given

04

limit

05

advertising

As demonstrated by answering these questions, students often need to look for synonyms in the text.

As stated in the information section, the hardest part of this type of question is probably understanding when the information is Not Given. It is important that students do not base any of the answers on their existing knowledge. All questions relate directly to the information in the text.

06 Tell students to read the short text on *Birthdays* and then answer the questions, which follow. This reading may tempt students to answer True or False, because the topic is well known. In several instances however, the information is actually Not Given in the text itself.

1 Not Given	2 False	3 True	4 Not Given
5 Not Given			

07-08 Tell students to complete Exercises 07 & 08, which aim to summarise the section on this task type.

07

1 rely	2 order	3 same	4 carefully
5 synonyms			

08

1 False	2 False	3 True	4 True	5 Not Given

GRAMMAR FOCUS: FIRST AND SECOND CONDITIONAL

This section of the lesson focuses on the first and second conditional. In terms of understanding a text, it is important that students know how they are used and their difference in meaning.

Ask students to re-read the first line of the text on Chinese Festivals.

If I could visit any country to be part of their celebrations and festivals, it would be China.

Elicit from students the following:

Does the speaker think they are likely to visit China? (No)

Which tense is used? First or second conditional? Why? (second conditional, as the speaker is not expecting to visit China.)

Ask students to discuss which country they would like to visit for its celebrations and why? For example:

If I could visit any country to be part of their celebrations and festivals it would be Brazil. They have amazing street parties and everyone gets dressed up.

09-10 Tell students to complete Exercises 09 & 10.

09

1 b	2 a	3 a: first conditional
b: second conditional		5 present simple
6 infinitive	7 past simple	8 would

10

1 go, will be	2 had, would/'d go	3 have, will/'ll
4 had, would/'d	5 wears, will/'ll	

EXAM SKILLS

11 Tell students to read the text and answer the questions, which follow.

1 False	2 Not Given	3 False	4 False
5 False	6 Not Given	7 True	

Engage students in a whole class discussion of their answers. Have them justify why they have chosen certain answers and aim to arrive at a class consensus.

WRITING

OUTCOMES

- identify and approach a 'problems and solutions' essay question
- plan and write an essay answering both parts of the question
- write a suitable introduction and conclusion
- revise past, present and future tenses.

OUTCOMES

This lesson focuses on the "problems and solutions" essay task, which can feature in Part 2 of the Writing exam. In this type of task, students are given a problem and required to produce several solutions. This task type can be expressed in several different ways, so this lesson teaches students how to recognise and answer it.

The aims of the lesson also include teaching/practising with students how to structure this type of essay and write a suitable introduction and conclusion.

LEAD-IN

01 Examples of the type of problems, students may be asked to write about, are given in Exercise 01 and relate to the unit topic, *Festivals and Traditions*. Ask students to discuss solutions to statements 1-5 in pairs. If needed, discuss one of the statements as a whole class and draw a mind map on the board illustrating possible solutions.

E.g.

Nowadays many children do not appreciate the presents they are given.

Do not give children too may gifts.

Limit present giving to birthdays/Christmas/ special occasions.

Parents should teach children to always say thank you and perhaps make thank you cards

Monitor the pair work by walking round and making notes of any interesting solutions and share these with the whole class afterwards.

02 Exercise 02 gives students important advice on how to handle this task type. Tell students to put a tick next to the good advice and a cross next to the bad advice.

Good advice:			
2 a	3 a	4 b	5 a

Discuss the answers with the whole class to ensure there is consensus about what constitutes good advice.

This section of the lesson concentrates on helping students structure their essay, as this is key component to achieving a good mark. Tell students to read the title carefully and then skim read the sample answer.

In order to give students practice at answering this type of question, they could do the following instead:

read the question carefully and underline the key words

discuss the question in pairs and brainstorm ideas

whole class feedback.

04 Students could then read the sample answer and complete the task on structuring

Tell students to complete exercise 04, by matching descriptions a-e with each section.

In order to make this task more interactive for students, you could enlarge the sample answer, delete the headings (introduction, main body etc..) and cut out the five different sections. Give each pair of students a copy of the five sections and ask them to order the answer.

Introduction: e

Main body: d, c, b

Conclusion: a

05 This exercise focuses on writing a good introduction and conclusion. Making sure an essay starts and finishes well is essential, as it has a significant impact on the examiner's impression of a student's essay.

Tell students to answer questions 1 & 2, which focus on the introduction.

1 too much about spending money → dominated by shops and companies … large profits; could be done to change the situation → offer some solutions

2 I will discuss some of the problems … also offer some solutions

Advice

As demonstrated in questions 1 & 2, in the introduction students must rephrase the question and give an indication of what will be discussed. Students may need practise at rephrasing the question, as this is sometimes challenging.

Tell students to complete questions 3-6, which focus on the conclusion.

3 the second, third and fourth paragraphs

4 No

5 No

6 a recommendation

Draw students' attention to Tip 5, stating that it is a good idea to include a prediction or recommendation in the conclusion of this essay type. In order to clarify the meaning of each, write the following on the board:

I do not think you should spend too much money on gifts at Christmas- (recommendation)

Eventually people will stop sending cards in the post and everything will be done online (prediction)

Ask students if they can think of any other predictions/recommendations associated with the unit topic.

06 Exercise 06 looks at the various ways in which this essay type can be phrased/expressed. It is important that students are aware of this, so they do not panic in the exam or waste time trying to identify the essay type.

1 suggest measures which could be taken to solve this problem

suggest ways in which these issues might be tackled

what can be done to minimise these bad effects?

how could these problems be solved?

2 issues, negative aspects, bad effects

3 D because it asks you to describe the reasons behind the problems

07 In this exercise students focus on grammatical accuracy and using the correct tenses.

Tell students to read the sample answer and complete it using the correct form of the verbs in the box. If needed, complete the first gap as a whole class.

1 (will / shall) discuss   2 is given   3 close
4 has passed   5 want   6 do
7 be ignored

Extension

In preparation for the exam task, you could ask students to discuss what was good about this answer. Students need to think about the following: structure, clarity of ideas, use of vocabulary, grammatical range and accuracy.

EXAM SKILLS

08 Give students this timed exam task. Remind or elicit from students the following:

they must allow time for planning at the beginning and checking at the end

they must read the question carefully and make sure their answer is relevant

they must include a strong introduction and conclusion

their ideas must be expressed clearly using an easy to follow structure

Sample answer

Planning a large family event or celebration can be a stressful experience. There are lots of things to consider and you need to make sure the plan for the event is successfully communicated to everyone. In the following essay I will describe some of the problems you may encounter and suggest ways in which these may be solved or avoided.

Planning a large event is perhaps difficult enough when you do not know the people attending the celebration. When you *do* know the people coming, however, the task can be even harder. For example, when organising an event for your family, your guests might have very particular views on how they expect the event to be; what you should be eating and how the decorations should be done.

Secondly, because it is a family event, you will need to provide food and entertainment for different age groups. You may have very young children attending, together with your elderly grandparents.

The solution to these problems is careful planning. You need to plan early and make sure you have all the information you need to organise your event. You will need to know exactly who is coming so the dietary requirements of both young and old can be catered for. You could also ask for opinions on the event during the planning stages, so your guests feel more included.

In conclusion, organising a large family event can be problematic. Nevertheless, if you plan carefully and include relatives during the preparation stage, all should go well.

LISTENING

OUTCOMES

This unit focuses on helping students with table and summary completion tasks. In order to answer these questions successfully, students must be able to read and identify the key information. This lesson teaches students how to interpret the text/data they are given, before listening to the recording.

LEAD-IN

01 Draw students' attention to the pictures and ask them to look at the table of events and match one of the events to each picture.

Clarify that students understand the different events and then ask them which they would prefer to attend and why. This will introduce and engage them in the topic of the listening.

Tell students to listen to the recording and complete Exercise 01. With weaker students, you might stop after each speaker and discuss the key facts which helped students to arrive at their answers.

Tapescript 68

Speaker 1: So, in conclusion, we can say that, despite the difficulties we had at the beginning, we managed to complete the programme over the three days without any further problems. In total, ten thousand attended the three days and feedback suggests that the events were exciting and produced true champions, especially the athletics events. Next year we'll have more money, so we're going to add new events to increase the competition and participation levels.

Speaker 2: It's clear, then, that the events didn't go as well as originally planned, so we will have to rethink our arrangements for next year. Clearly, a large tent in the college grounds is not ideal for an event of this type if we're hit by bad weather again, as we were with this year's event. This caused a lot of problems with the preparation of the dishes and the display of the produce from different parts of the world. It also meant that visitors couldn't really get a chance to try everything on display. As a result, much of it went to waste, which is something we have to avoid next time.

Speaker 3: One of the main issues that we had with this event was that the main attraction, Paul Simmons, had to cancel at the last minute as he'd been suffering from a serious throat infection for a week and hadn't managed to recover in time. As a result, we had to find another act, and managed to get Nicky Munroe at very short notice. She performed magnificently, the audience loved her and that saved the festival I would say. Everyone agreed that she has an amazing vocal range.

Speaker 4: The most successful aspect of the event was the variety of products that were on offer. It's wonderful to see students being so creative. We saw practical applications that'll make significant developments in education and even business if they go into production, as well as very entertaining ideas, especially the robot football game. I'm pleased to say that our college team won!

Speaker 5: I'm sure you'll all agree when I say that the quality of the talks and performances over the last three days was very high. The talk given by the top novelist, Henry Peters, on effective plotting and characterisation was excellent, and the audience will have learnt a great deal to help them with planning and writing their future works. What's more, the quality of verse produced in the workshops was very high, and we hope to run that again next time with greater overall participation.

Speaker 6: While there were some wonderful and fascinating works on display, I felt that there wasn't enough variety. Unfortunately, this was because of the limited exhibition space we had. This meant that we could only have one room for portraits and another for landscapes. We hope to extend that next year into other forms, such as still life and abstract, but we'll have to see what rooms are available. We also hope to install clay ovens next year to give our students the chance to create their own pottery and display it for the visitors.

Music festival: 3
Arts and crafts festival: 6
Poetry and literature festival: 5
Food festival: 2
Sports festival: 1
Technology fair: 4

Alternative

Ask students to listen again and make a note of the key words, which gave them the correct answer.

This section of the lesson discusses the summary completion task, which may feature in the listening. Draw students' attention to the information box, stating what the task is and how students should approach it.

02 Tell students to complete Exercise 02 and draw students' attention to Tip 2, stating that the information in the recording is in the same order as the summary. With weaker groups you might focus students' attention on the overall context and the specific details that they will need to listen out for.

Tapescript 69

Dr Saunders: Hello everybody. Welcome to this meeting to review this year's arts festival. As you know, this is the fourth and biggest festival that we've run at the university and it's clear now that it's fast becoming a fixture in the calendar of the city and the county and attracting attention from the rest of the country, as well as from abroad. First of all, I'd like to review the preparations for the festival, then go on to do an analysis of the festival itself and how well it went. The plan is then for you to work in teams of three, with one tutor and two students in each team, and for you to discuss the festival in more detail so you can come up with suggestions for the organising committee to consider for next year's festival.

Well, as I said, we're in our fourth year and we added some new events. The first festival focused mainly on music and the performing arts, as it was felt that those would be the best types of event for both students and the public to take part in. More forms of art, in particular short films and photography, were added over the next two years and this year we have extended our offer to include painting and crafts, with a particular focus on the students here producing their own work, both for exhibition and competition. This was largely successful, but I'll discuss that in detail later. We also invited professional artists in some of the fields to perform, and that will be something for you to review for the next event. What was particularly encouraging this year, was that we had contributions to the festival from the highest number of students to date, with representatives from every nationality at the university.

As in previous years, we planned to use the spare university accommodation for all the visitors, both students and non-students, but as we expected a greater attendance at this year's festival, we also arranged accommodation at the city college three miles from here and arranged coach transfers between the college and the university campus. Unfortunately, that

proved problematic and we won't repeat those arrangements next year. We also arranged the catering both here and at the city college and one of the new ideas we tried was to experiment with dishes based on different regional themes over the five days. This allowed our international students … well, the keen cooks among them anyway … to create the menus and work with the catering company to produce breakfast, lunch and dinner.

Of course, one of the main aims of this festival, apart from the obvious ones of extending the university's reputation and giving our students the chance to take part in a wonderful event, was to help develop our young people's organisational skills and give them some experience of real work, mostly as volunteers. Of course, we had to pay for professional organisers to make sure the festival ran well, but as our money was limited and we wanted to give as many opportunities to our students as possible, we made sure that they ran all of the events themselves under the direction of the professionals and, of course, alongside the tutors.

1 painting and crafts	2 students
3 catering	4 volunteers

03 Exercise 03 gives students an example of summary completion task. Before they listen to the recording, ask students to do the following in pairs:

Skim read the text to identify the topic.

Underline key word.

Predict the missing information and identify what type of word is missing (adjective, noun etc.).

If necessary, complete the first gap as a whole class.

E.g. The _____ event was the most popular with many different entries.

Answer could be noun and/or adjective

Tell students to listen to the recording and complete the summary using up to two words and/or a number.

Tapescript 70

Dr Saunders: So, now let me turn to the actual event and how it went. As I said, we had the biggest offer of arts events in the four years we've been running the festival. In total, the number of visitors over the whole five days was 12,500, which is a 10% increase on the previous year and just over three times the number in the first year that we held it. This clearly shows that we're going in the right direction by expanding the variety of events on offer. The short film event at the university cinema was the best attended, with entries from a wide variety of nationalities here at the university on a number of fascinating topics. I think we can all agree that the quality was excellent, as was the standard of the photography exhibition and the paintings in the art gallery. Our feedback from students and visitors was very positive.

However, there are three issues that we should address in our discussions. First, Wayne Rogers, our headline music act, had to call off two days before the event due to illness and we didn't have time to find another act. Needless to say, all those who bought tickets for the main concert were disappointed and we had to return their money. We need to discuss suggestions for avoiding this in the future. Also, while we had some good crafts on display, especially the clothes, pottery, sculptures and glass objects, the exhibition was poorly attended, so we have to decide if it needs to be changed or perhaps reduced in some way. The last issue involves the art gallery and, in particular, security. Although we had attendants on duty all the time, three paintings were stolen, much to the disappointment of the artists who painted them. They were valued at around £3,000 in total, and the artists had expected to be able to sell them in the future, so we need to look into this and think about how we can increase security for next year, while also avoiding any unnecessary inconvenience for our visitors.

Regarding the arrangements for accommodation and catering, generally things went well, but there were some issues with the accommodation in the city college. As there were a lot of late bookings, we had to provide more accommodation than we originally planned to do, with the result that some people ended up in accommodation of a lower standard than they expected. We apologised to them and gave them back part of their payments, but we need to avoid this issue in the future, especially as the festival is growing and we don't want to harm our reputation. Another issue was that, at certain times of the day, there were not enough volunteers on hand to help visitors, so we'll need to make sure that we organise the availability of volunteers better next time. On the other hand, the transport that we organised was excellent and the catering was highly appreciated, in terms of both variety and quality. So, I'd like you to think of more ideas to extend the catering opportunities for next year.

The last thing I want to focus on now is how much we spent. As I said earlier, we had budgeted for £50,000 to organise the event and expected £50,000 in earnings from the event, but the final balance sheet showed that the event made just over £90,000, so we have some money to go into the budget for next year, which is an excellent result. However, I feel there are still some areas where we could cut our spending and perhaps reduce charges for visitors. Many of the volunteers felt that some of the paid helpers that we brought in to supervise the activities were not really worth the expense. They felt that some of them did very little for what we paid them and others didn't really organise some of the events that well, so I would welcome suggestions on improving organisation while saving money. Also, I feel that another good way of raising funds is to get more business support from local companies, who could help the festival grow by sponsoring events and advertising their products and services more around the festival. Now I'd like to turn to …

1	short film	2	poorly / badly attended
3	three / 3 paintings	4	low(er) / poor(er) standard / quality
5	paid helpers	6	business support

04 Exercises 04 & 05 deal with the task type, which requires students to complete tables with words from the recording. As stated in the information section, the key to this task, is for students read the table carefully before listening to the recording. As with any completion task, students must try to predict what type of information is missing before attempting the listening.

Tapescript 71

Dr Reynolds: So, first of all, we need to look at the events and see what should be included in next year's festival and what changes should be made. Dr Saunders mentioned that there were issues with the music and crafts. What are your feelings on those two issues? Do you want to start, Sangita?

Sangita: Well, as regards the music, I think we need to have another artist in reserve in case the main act can't perform, like in this year's festival. It doesn't have to be a well-known band. It could be a small act, like a student band. What do you think, Lawrence?

Lawrence: You have a point, but I'm not really sure if any artists would be happy to perform only if the main act lets us down. In any case, how often does that happen? This was the first time, and I don't see it happening again in the future.

Dr Reynolds: I'm not sure we can take that for granted, Lawrence. If you look at what happened, we lost £3,000 as we had to return money to the audience. I don't think anything bad would have happened, but I think we need to bear in mind that our visitors are the most important aspect of the festival and we have to make sure we keep them happy at all costs.

Lawrence: How about we arrange the programme so that on one night there isn't a famous headline act but a good local band, so that we can change the programme to make them the main act if anyone else isn't able to perform. We could put them on the last evening, and tell them that they may be needed on the other evenings, just in case. That way, we're helping good local talent and making sure that our visitors are happy.

Sangita: Yes, I can see that working. Then we could use the student band to play the last night if we have to switch the local band from the last night to an earlier night.

Dr Reynolds: OK ... good ideas. I'll make a note so that we can take it back to the organising committee. Now, let's move on to the question of crafts. As we heard, the event didn't go very well and lacked visitors. What do you think we should do, Sangita?

Sangita: Well, I have a personal interest in this. I've been creating my own fashion designs and I had some clothes on display mixing Western and Indian themes. Actually, I spent some time watching the visitors and I thought they liked clothes a lot. I think we have to be careful to distinguish the clothes from the other crafts.

Lawrence: Yes, I noticed that. I spent the third day in the craft section helping visitors and I noticed that the clothes exhibition was the most appreciated. I think the glass and ceramic section had hardly any visitors when I was there. Perhaps we should just have the clothes on display, maybe even extend that section?

Dr Reynolds: Yes, that could be a good solution. I don't think we should get rid of the glass and pottery altogether, but I certainly think we should promote the clothes section more.

Lawrence: Well, here's a suggestion: we could even think of turning that into a separate fashion show. What do you think of that?

Sangita: Good idea! I was thinking about that anyway. Can we put that to the committee?

Dr Reynolds: Of course. I've made a note of it. Regarding the theatre and poetry, do you think we need to make any changes?

Lawrence: Nothing major, I don't think, but perhaps we should use at least one day to present new plays and poems by our own students. It's wonderful putting on plays by well-known

playwrights and readings of well-known poets, but perhaps we should promote our own talent here in the university. It would certainly help the performing arts students to expand their coursework, and we could have a competition for the best new works.

Dr Reynolds: Excellent idea, Lawrence. What do you think, Sangita?

Sangita: Yes, but let's not limit it to just English. We could also have performances from our international students in their languages. I think that would really help promote the festival as an international event.

Dr Reynolds: Fine. We can propose that as well. And as far as the photography and cinema sections are concerned, they'll keep expanding.

Lawrence: Well, personally, I don't think the quality of the photography exhibition was very high. I think there are issues with digital photography being presented as a printed exhibition. You can never really capture the true meaning of the photograph like that. I would suggest just having digital displays, you know, tablets that visitors can use to see the photographer's collection. That way, it'll encourage photographers to develop their ideas and think about their exhibits almost as films with a story. I think that's the way photography is going these days.

Sangita: I don't agree. I think each image should be appreciated in its own way, as the photographer intends. I don't think we should push photographers into one direction. That said, I think the idea of having tablets and digital screens is a good idea if we can afford it. Perhaps we could have two sections – digital displays and non-digital displays.

Dr Reynolds: Sounds good, Sangita. I can certainly put that to the committee and see if they'll consider it. So, if that's all about the events themselves, I'd like to discuss the organisation of the festival ...

1 Student band	2 Book local band for the last night
3 Show only clothes	4 Have students' plays and poems
5 Have digital and non-digital photographs displayed	

05 Tell students to read the table in Exercise 05 carefully. As stated in Tip 5, students should focus on the different categories in order to decide what information is missing. For example, elicit from students which speaker will give them the answer to question 1. (Sangita)

Tapescript 72

Dr Reynolds: Now, the next thing I think we should discuss is the accommodation situation. It seems clear that the number of visitors is set to grow, so we need to have a suitable plan in place to deal with the

Lawrence: Actually, I saw the accommodation that we used at the city college, and it was pretty basic, though it was clean and tidy. There was only a bed and a desk in each room. Another thing the visitors complained about was the lack of Wi-Fi in the rooms, especially as they'd paid for rooms with Wi-Fi. It certainly wasn't ideal.

Dr Reynolds: Do you have anything to add, Sangita?

Sangita: Yeah … I can understand why they weren't happy. I'd have felt the same in their position.

Dr Reynolds: Well, there's that new holiday development at Elm Park, quite close to the university. Perhaps we could use their rooms. After all, it won't be the holiday high season, so there should be plenty of empty rooms that we could use.

Sangita: That's true. How about taking over some of their rooms and advertising them as accommodation specifically for families with children? They're going to have an outdoor and an indoor adventure area for young people. We had quite a few teenagers this year coming with their parents. If we can attract more by offering them the facilities at the holiday park in a special package, they can go there if they get bored with the festival.

Lawrence: Excellent idea! They'll be around 15 or 16 years old and when they come to the festival, they'll get an idea of what it'd be like to study here. I'm sure it'll help our future prospects as a university.

Dr Reynolds: I agree. I'll be happy to present those ideas to the committee. Moving on to the catering, it seems clear that the idea of theme days with different kinds of national and regional dishes went down very well. I'll recommend repeating it next year, but do you have anything else to say about the catering?

Sangita: Not really … one thing is maybe we could tell the students about the festival earlier in the year and invite them to suggest themes and also to volunteer their own cooking skills to help with it. I think that'll make sure that we vary what we offer from year to year, so that we don't just repeat the same dishes each time.

Lawrence: But we should always have fish and chips on the menu! We can't do without that! Seriously though, I agree.

Dr Reynolds: OK. I'll make a note of that as well. Moving on to the helpers, you were both directly involved in that. Do you think it was a good idea to get professionals for the organising?

Lawrence: In a word, 'no'. I think the ones that I worked with didn't really know what they were doing. We were paying them a lot to do their work, but I don't think they really took it as seriously as they should have. They were thinking it was just a student event. On more than one occasion, some of the volunteers had to take charge and make sure that the events went smoothly.

Sangita: Yes, you're right. That was my experience as well. We ended up paying them a lot of money for poor service. It was one of the reasons why there were too few volunteers at some events – because the organisation was so poor. I think the idea of bringing back former students is a good idea. At least then we can be more certain that they know about the university and they'll probably be more committed to doing a good job.

Dr Reynolds: I think you're both right. I was disappointed and I think former students will be a great improvement, so I'll note that as well. We need to talk about finance, but before that, I just want to mention the issue of security. Thinking about the stolen paintings, what do you think we should do about that?

Lawrence: I'm not really sure. I mean, we had the university security guards on duty the whole time, so I don't think we can really add to that.

Sangita: Well, I noticed on more than one occasion that there were windows open in some rooms which made it easy for people to climb in and steal things. I think the main thing is to remind students and volunteers that it's their personal responsibility to be careful and look out for any security issues. So if one of us sees an open window, we should either check with security why it's open, or simply close it.

Dr Reynolds: You're right, Sangita. I'm sure the committee is aware of this, but I'll note it just to show that we've given it some thought. Now finance – what are your feelings on Dr Saunders' suggestions about sponsorship?

Lawrence: I don't think that will go down too well with most students. I mean, personally, I'm not against it, but I think students generally won't be very keen to have businesses involved in what they see as their arts festival. I'm sure they'll be happy to take part in more events to raise money throughout the year before the festival, but they won't be happy about big businesses taking over and having their names all over the university.

Sangita: Well, I think it's going to happen anyway. Everything is commercial to some extent these days. I don't think it's a bad idea, as long as it's done in good taste. I think any businesses that do want to sponsor us or advertise should be aware that they need to work closely with us and respect the spirit of the festival.

Lawrence: Perhaps we could involve local businesses as well as national ones that don't just put their name on the festival, but can actually sponsor specific events, award prizes, and so on. So, for example, a local cinema could sponsor the short film event and even send along a representative to judge the films, that sort of thing.

Dr Reynolds: Yes, I see what you mean. In that way, they'll be directly involved in the festival, which will encourage them to take an active part and build up their reputations for supporting the arts. Well, thank you both. We have a lot of useful suggestions to take back to the committee.

1 families	2 cooking	3 professionals
4 responsibility	5 prizes	

EXAM SKILLS

06 This sample exam task practises table completion. Before asking students to complete the task, elicit from students what they should be doing before listening to the recording.

Tell students to complete the table in Exercise 06, using no more than three words and/ or a number.

Tapescript 73

Dr Reynolds: Hello Dr Saunders. I just want to tell you about the suggestions that Lawrence and Sangita made during our discussion and see what you think.

Dr Saunders: Thanks, yes. Please do.

Dr Reynolds: First of all, regarding the music, they think that it might be a good idea to have a good local band who can replace the main act if it has to let us down at the last minute, which is what happened this year. The band could be scheduled for later in the week on the understanding that they might have to play on an earlier night. We could also have one evening with a student band.

Dr Saunders: Well, it sounds good in theory to plan a rearrangement, but I think it would be too complicated to arrange. We would depend too much on all the bands being able to play on any of the nights. I think it's simpler just to give the audience a refund if it happens again. But I'm happy to have one evening

supporting local bands and student bands, as that's the main point of the festival – to encourage people to take part.

Dr Reynolds: The next thing is the crafts. They felt that a fashion show would be a good way of expanding the clothes exhibition, and that perhaps we should reduce or even get rid of the glass and pottery exhibition.

Dr Saunders: Well, first of all, I think that the fashion show is a good idea as it can help the international students to get involved in more activities and develop their ideas with clothes. But I'm not keen to get rid of the glass and pottery exhibitions completely, as it's important for the university to be seen to encourage all forms of art and not just the most popular ones, so we should keep that for the time being.

Dr Reynolds: OK ... now ... regarding theatre and poetry, they felt that it would be good for students to write and perform their own plays and poetry, as well as those by famous playwrights and poets.

Dr Saunders: That sounds like an excellent idea! It'd help a lot to raise standards in writing and performance. I'd love to see that taking place.

Dr Reynolds: Also on that topic, there was a feeling that works in other languages should be encouraged.

Dr Saunders: Most certainly. That would help the international students feel far more at home and valued as part of the university.

Dr Reynolds: There was one other event we discussed, and that was photography. It was felt that we should have both digital and non-digital exhibits.

Dr Saunders: I don't think we could manage that, at least not yet. Quality tablets and screens would be too expensive, especially with the number we'd have to buy, so it's not an option for next year because of the high cost.

Dr Reynolds: OK ... as for the accommodation and the catering, they felt that we could use the holiday park that's being built nearby, and we should encourage students to take a greater part in cooking and helping with the catering.

Dr Saunders: Well, first, I know for a fact that the new holiday park is not likely to be completed by festival time next year as they've run into trouble with the building, but we could certainly think about it in the future. I do like the idea of the students having a greater role in the catering and cooking, as it will clearly be helpful for their all-round development.

Dr Reynolds:	OK. The next thing is the professional organisers. They felt that the standard was quite low and that the volunteers didn't experience good leadership from them. They think it would be better to ask former students to work as organisers, as they'd be more familiar with the university and more committed, too.
Dr Saunders:	I appreciate that, but unfortunately that wouldn't work. It'd be too much trouble trying to find them and get them employed. However, I think we should review the organisers that we used this year and have a much better selection system in place for the next festival.
Dr Reynolds:	Now the last two points are about security and finance. As far as security goes, they think we should do more to encourage the students to take it seriously.
Dr Saunders:	I agree. If we can encourage students to be more aware of security, not just during the festival, it'd really help to increase trust among all our students because they'll be looking out for each other.
Dr Reynolds:	As for finance, they thought that, first, we could encourage students to help raise money throughout the year, and, secondly, we could encourage businesses to sponsor the events and advertise more, though it needs to be handled with care.
Dr Saunders:	Well, regarding sponsorship and advertising, the committee is already looking at the possibilities as it will encourage more interest in the activities that we do and also help our reputation generally. Unfortunately, I don't think asking the students to raise more money during the year is a good idea as we already have a programme in place for that and, if the students are involved any more, they'll spend less time on their studies and I don't want anything to disrupt those.

1 forms / types / kinds	2 standards	3 high cost
4 development	5 trust	
6 studies / studying / (academic) work / course(s)		

SPEAKING

OUTCOMES

- speak in detail about celebrations and special events
- make comparisons between the past and the present, or between similarities and differences
- use words and phrases that show 'concession' to look at both sides of an argument
- stress key words to comparisons.

OUTCOMES

This unit teaches students how to speak in detail about celebrations and special events which is a topic, which could arise in any part of the Speaking exam.

Outcomes 2,3 & 4 focus on Part 3 of the exam in which students may be asked to make comparisons or present both sides of an argument.

LEAD-IN

01 In all parts of the speaking exam, students could be asked to describe or answer questions on festivals and traditions, particularly relating to their own country.

In order to prepare students for this, Exercise 01 ask them to discuss typical exam type questions..

Tell students to discuss questions 1-4 in pairs.

Extension

Ask students to think of other questions, related to this topic.

E.g. How did you celebrate your last birthday? What is your favourite celebration and why? Do you know people who don't like celebrating? Why? Why not?

You could then write all the questions on the board and ask students to practise answering them. For variety, tell students to swap partners or present this as a whole class mingling activity.

This section of the lesson discusses Part 3 of the exam, when students could be asked to compare the importance of a topic in the past and present. Tell students to read an example of this in the information box. As also stated here, it is important that students discuss both sides of the argument in their answer. Exercise 02 focuses on this aspect of the task.

02 Tell students to complete Exercise 02 by completing each of the statements. If needed, complete the first as a whole class.

Sample answer

Celebrations were important in the past because
    a people were usually all together as a family.
    b celebrations were not always about money.

Celebrations are important now because
    a we spend a lot of money on them.
    b it is harder for families to get together all the time.

Celebrations were not important in the past because
    a people had to work longer hours and had less time to celebrate.
    b people had less money to spend on celebrating.

Celebrations are not important now because
    a some smaller celebrations are no longer celebrated.
    b the focus is only on money and not the meaning of the event.

03 Tell students to complete Exercise 03 and draw their attention to Tip 3, stating that their answers should be detailed and include a range of tenses.

> **Sample answers in bold.**
>
> 1 Well, on the one hand, we still spend a lot of money every year on celebrations – and it seems like we spend more every year! On the other hand, it could be that some of the smaller public holidays and events are becoming less important as everyone is too focused on the bigger ones. I also think that in the past celebrations were more important because they were less about money and more about the meaning behind the event.
>
> 2 I think celebrations are more important now than they were in the past. Because people work longer hours and sometimes live far from where they grew up, it is hard for families to get together all the time. While celebrations were also important in the past because we were all together as a family, I think that they are even more meaningful now as we cannot take meeting our loved ones for granted.

04 This exercise explains to students that another useful way of making comparisons is using, "would." Write the following examples on the board.

In the past, people would spend less money on birthdays and Christmas.

In the past, people used to spend less money on birthdays and Christmas.

In these examples both *would* and *used to* are used to describe past habits.

Ask students if they can think of other examples related to festivals and celebrations. Collate good ideas on the board.

05 As mentioned in Exercise 02, it is important that students consider both sides of the argument, when presented with this type of question. Exercise 05 gives students some key vocabulary which can be used to express different points of view.

Draw students' attention to the information box, which gives some examples of this type of phrase: although, even though, while etc..

Tell students to complete Exercise 05 and draw their attention to Tip 5, providing further similar expressions.

06 Another aspect students could be asked to discuss, is talking about similarities and differences. Exercises 06, 07 and 08 practise this idea of making comparisons.

08 Tell students to look at the adjectives in the box. Adjectives are key when comparing and contrasting, so it is important they have a good knowledge of these.

Elicit the meaning of any unknown words.

Draw students' attention to Tip 8, stating the difference between *compare* and *contrast*. This is important for students to understand as they could be asked to do either or both in the exam. Try to elicit or feed examples of comparing and contrasting and collate them on the board.

09 This exercise focuses on word stress in order to emphasise difference when speaking.

Tell students to listen to the sentences and underline the words which the speakers stress.

Tapescript and answers 74

> 1 I prefer spending time with my family on my **birthday** rather than spending time with them at **New Year**.
>
> 2 **This** holiday is much more exciting than **that** holiday.
>
> 3 **These** ideas might be better for a celebration than **those** ideas.
>
> 4 **Some** people don't enjoy public holidays as much as **other** people I know.

10 Tell students to complete Exercise 10 individually and then work together in pairs to practise stressing key words. Go round and monitor and support. Write up good examples on the board, if appropriate.

EXAM SKILLS

11-12 This sample exam task gives students practice in all parts of the exam.

Tell students to complete Exercises 11 & 12 in pairs.

13 Exercise 13 provides students with an example of how Part 3 could be answered in this case.

Tapescript 75

Examiner:	What is the difference between how people celebrate special events today compared with the past?
Student:	Well, I think that in the past people would spend a long time preparing food or going shopping for presents, but now people tend to eat out and order their presents online. While this might seem more convenient, perhaps making an effort is part of what makes the festivals so important. I think we're losing that now.
Examiner:	Should we learn about the special events of other countries in school?
Student:	I certainly think we should find out as much as possible about how people in other countries live. However, I'm not sure we need to introduce all international festivals into our calendar, as people might think less of our own important festivals and culture.

Examiner: What will special events be like in the future?

Student: I think as people are getting busier, fewer events will continue to be celebrated, as people just don't have the time to celebrate all of them. On the other hand, we might also see an increase in online-only events, where family members don't travel to their parents' house but instead wish them Happy New Year or something over webchat software. That way, although people might live far away from each other, they can still celebrate over video chat.

Examiner: Do we spend too much money on special events like Valentine's Day or birthdays?

Student: I'm not so sure about that. I think we've always spent lots of money on those things, although obviously some people do like to spend more than others. Anyway, I don't think it's the money, but the thought that counts.

Tell students to practise the same questions in pairs.

Alternative

After the listening, students could discuss why they thought the candidate did well.